ALTERNATIVES TO PRISON
REHABILITATION AND OTHER PROGRAMS

Incarceration Issues:
Punishment, Reform, and Rehabilitation

TITLE LIST

ALTERNATIVES TO PRISON
REHABILITATION AND OTHER PROGRAMS

by Craig Russell

Mason Crest Publishers
Philadelphia

Mason Crest Publishers Inc.
370 Reed Road
Broomall, Pennsylvania 19008
(866) MCP-BOOK (toll free)

2 3 4 5 6 7 8 9 10

Library of Congress Cataloging-in-Publication Data

Russell, Craig.
  Alternatives to prison : rehabilitation and other programs / by Craig Russell.
     p. cm.
  Includes index.
  ISBN 1-59084-991-4   ISBN 1-59084-984-1 (series)
  ISBN 978-1-59084-991-0   ISBN 9781-59084-984-2 (series)

  1. Alternatives to imprisonment—United States. 2. Criminals—Rehabilitation—United States. 3. Corrections—United States. I. Title.
  HV9304.R87 2005
  364.6'0973—dc22
                    2005005564

Interior design by MK Bassett-Harvey.
Interiors produced by Harding House Publishing Service, Inc.
www.hardinghousepages.com

Cover design by Peter Spires Culotta.

Printed in Malaysia by Times Offset (M) Sdn.Bhd.

CONTENTS

INTRODUCTION

by Larry E. Sullivan, Ph.D.

Prisons will be with us as long as we have social enemies. We will punish them for acts that we consider criminal, and we will confine them in institutions.

Prisons have a long history, one that fits very nicely in the religious context of sin, evil, guilt, and expiation. In fact, the motto of one of the first prison reform organizations was "Sin no more." Placing offenders in prison was, for most of the history of the prison, a ritual for redemption through incarceration; hence the language of punishment takes on a very theological cast. The word "penitentiary" itself comes from the religious concept of penance. When we discuss prisons, we are dealing not only with the law but with very strong emotions and reactions to acts that range from minor or misdemeanor crimes to major felonies like murder and rape.

Prisons also reflect the level of the civilizing process through which a culture travels, and it tells us much about how we treat our fellow human beings. The great nineteenth-century Russian author Fyodor Dostoyevsky, who was a political prisoner, remarked, "The degree of civilization in a society can be measured by observing its prisoners." Similarly, Winston Churchill, the great British prime minister during World War II, said that the "treatment of crime and criminals is one of the most unfailing tests of civilization of any country."

Since the very beginnings of the American Republic, we have attempted to improve and reform the way we imprison criminals. For much of the history of the American prison, we tried to rehabilitate or modify the criminal behavior of offenders through a variety of treatment programs. In the last quarter of the twentieth century, politicians and citizens alike realized that this attempt had failed, and we began passing stricter laws, imprisoning people for longer terms and building more prisons. This movement has taken a great toll on society. Approximately two million people are behind bars today. This movement has led to the

overcrowding of prisons, worse living conditions, fewer educational programs, and severe budgetary problems. There is also a significant social cost, since imprisonment splits families and contributes to a cycle of crime, violence, drug addiction, and poverty.

All these are reasons why this series on incarceration issues is extremely important for understanding the history and culture of the United States. Readers will learn all facets of punishment: its history; the attempts to rehabilitate offenders; the increasing number of women and juveniles in prison; the inequality of sentencing among the races; attempts to find alternatives to incarceration; the high cost, both economically and morally, of imprisonment; and other equally important issues. These books teach us the importance of understanding that the prison system affects more people in the United States than any institution, other than our schools.

ALTERNATIVES TO PRISON

CHAPTER 1.

WHY DO WE NEED ALTERNATIVES TO PRISON?

In 1967, when he was sixteen years old, George B. stole $60,000. He didn't steal it all at once, though. Instead, he took it a little at a time: fifty dollars here, a hundred dollars there. Sometimes he got it by robbing strangers. If he saw someone walking down a Manhattan street looking a little scared, he would push her up against the nearest wall and threaten to hurt her if she didn't give up her money. George was six feet tall and weighed about 250 pounds—and since he only picked on people smaller than him, no one fought back. He had never, he said, been in a fight in his life.

Drugs are a costly habit.

He got most of that money, though, from stealing and then cashing people's Social Security checks. He knew what day the post office delivered the checks, he knew what color they were as he peered into the locked mailboxes, and he knew how to use a stick and a little chewed gum to slide the envelope up out of the mail slot. He also knew how to get the checks cashed at some of the numerous check-cashing businesses throughout New York City.

But he didn't use the money he stole to buy a fancy car or to live in luxury. Instead, he spent that money—all of it—on just one thing.

Heroin.

He lived like that for several years, stealing and robbing and getting high. Heroin was his only interest. It kept him warm, made him feel safe,

Paraphernalia for shooting heroin.

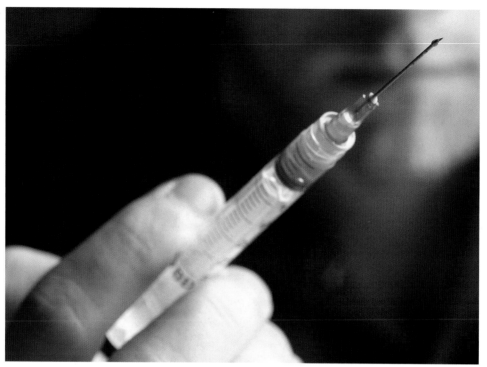
Heroin is a poor friend.

and gave him a reason to live. Back then, he said, heroin was his only friend.

One night in the early 1970s, George was shooting up on a Harlem street. He said he was so high that he didn't know he was high, so he kept jabbing the needle into his arm again and again and again. In his drugged-out haze, he didn't see the police officer until it was much too late. George was arrested and charged with heroin possession. Since he had just made a big buy and had a large amount on him, he was also charged with dealing heroin.

Things looked bad. But the judge didn't know George had stolen so much money. She didn't know that all those people had missed their Social Security checks. She only knew that George was young (he was just twenty years old at the time) and that he had never been in trouble with the law before. As a result, the judge gave him a choice: twenty years in Attica State Prison, or ***rehabilitation***.

George chose rehabilitation.

THE RENAISSANCE PROJECT

The Renaissance Project, which began more than thirty years ago, is just one of hundreds of substance abuse programs in the United States and Canada. Based in New York State's Westchester County, the program provides care, education, self-help, and support as it helps guide its clients to constructive lives. It has a hundred-bed inpatient facility in Ellendale, New York, as well as several outpatient facilities throughout the county. It also provides a twenty-four-hour telephone hotline and counseling services to the 1,200 people it helps every year.

First, he went through the Renaissance Project's substance abuse program and got himself off heroin. Then he went to Westchester Community College, where he got a degree as a *radiologist*. He got married and landed a job taking X-rays at a hospital in Beacon, New York. After his divorce, he went back to college but found that he didn't like it anymore. Instead, he traveled, first through the southwestern United States and then the Caribbean and Central America. He fell in love with Belize, a small, English-speaking country on the Yucatan Peninsula just southeast of Mexico. Eventually, he moved there permanently.

George B. enjoyed his life. He ate mostly fish and fruit and gave visitors guided tours of the Gulf of Mexico in his twenty-one-foot boat. In 1990, when he was forty years old, he died suddenly of a brain *aneurysm*.

Although he died young, George B. was one of the lucky ones. Instead of spending the last half of his life confined to prison, he spent it on the outside—learning, loving, and traveling. The judge had offered him an alternative to prison; taking it made all the difference in what remained of his life.

Most of us think that if we break the law and a jury convicts us, we will spend a certain amount of time in jail or prison. But that's not always true. Today, many convicted criminals are offered alternatives to prison. Some, like George B., might be given **probation** and sentenced to attend a drug rehabilitation program. Some go to jail or prison but are released early on **parole**. Some might be sentenced to community service and work (for free) for a government agency, perhaps, or a nonprofit organization. Others might be sent to a "boot camp," where they undergo military-style discipline. Still others receive "house arrest" and serve their sentence under **electronic surveillance** at home, or perhaps they're ordered to serve part-time at a day-reporting center.

THE NEED FOR ALTERNATIVES

Why are there so many alternatives to prison? One reason is simple practicality. The United States, for example, has almost three times as many prisoners as it did just twenty-five years ago. According to the U.S. Department of Justice, just under two million Americans were under correctional supervision in 1980. By 2003, that number had risen to almost seven million, and there just isn't enough prison space to have them all **incarcerated**.

Canada was facing the same sort of trouble in the mid-1990s. Its prison population was increasing at twice its former rate. But in 1996, the Canadian government changed its criminal code. These changes gave judges the ability to give more alternative sentences. As a result, Canada had fewer prisoners in 2002 than it did ten years earlier. "Not everybody has to go to jail," says David Daubney, who was the head of Canada's sentencing reform committee. "There are other ways of punishing people."

The cost of keeping someone in prison continues to rise as well. In 1988, Americans spent $20 billion on prisons. That was roughly ten times what they had spent just ten years earlier. The U.S. Department of Justice reported that in 2004, the day-to-day operations of all state prisons cost $28.4 billion dollars per year, an increase of $5.5 billion over 1996.

THE DIFFERENCE BETWEEN JAIL AND PRISON

Usually, when people are first arrested, they are put in jail. A jail is generally a small facility operated by the local county, city, or town. Unless they can afford bail or are released on just their promise that they will appear for all hearings, people are held in jail until their trials. Jails also hold people convicted of minor crimes. People convicted of major crimes are sent to prisons, which are usually much larger than jails. Most prisons are run by either a state government or by the federal government. Some prisons, however, are run by a business.

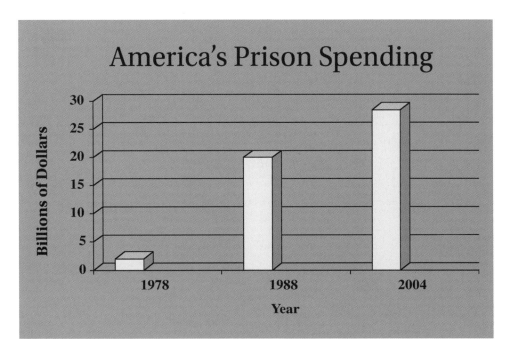

America's Prison Spending

Billions of Dollars vs Year

Prisons cost American taxpayers billions of dollars.

Between 1986 and 2001, state prison costs almost tripled, climbing from $11.7 billion per year to $29.5 billion per year. In other words, while it cost the average American $49 a year to keep one person in prison in 1986, it cost $104 a year to keep someone there in 2001. By 2005, it cost between $25,000 and $30,000 a year to keep one person in prison.

Although Canada has reduced the number of people in its prisons, the cost of keeping someone there continues to rise just as it does in the United States. It cost $189 Canadian per day, or nearly $69,000 a year (about $45,000 American) to keep one prisoner in a jail during 2001–2002, and this was a 3 percent increase over 1999–2000. As Graham Stewart of Canada's John Howard Society says, "We could put somebody through university for what we spend on a person in prison."

A second reason for alternatives to prison is that some people believe incarceration is ineffective; they think that prison just doesn't work. David Daubney says, "we know the jails are really just schools for crime." Much research shows that being sent to prison does little to prevent further crime.

THE HISTORY OF PUNISHMENT

Our modern prisons began as an alternative to earlier forms of punishment. Before the 1800s, prisons did not exist in the United States. Offenders were punished quickly and directly for their crimes. Punishments in colonial America varied widely and often depended on the amount of money a person had. The rich might be fined, and if they demonstrated good behavior, they might even get that money back. The poor, however, did not get off so easily, and their punishments could be extremely harsh. Thieves were often whipped and ordered to repay what they had stolen, sometimes at several times their value. Sometimes they were even branded with the letter T to warn others of what they had done. Drunks were often forced to repent in front of the members of the church. Some who swore received thirty-nine lashes, and some who had sex outside marriage were even hanged. Incarceration, at that time, did not exist.

The stocks were an early American form of imprisonment.

The American Revolution, however, changed the way people looked at the causes of crime and the effectiveness of punishment. Many Americans believed that the ideas that had inspired their successful revolution against England would lead to a new age, one of brotherhood and progress. Americans had reformed their government, and they would reform their view of crime and punishment as well.

Generally speaking, there were two kinds of reformers in the early 1800s. One group was called the *rationalists*. They believed the law should be rational—in other words, that it should make sense and be reasonable. They believed that people broke the law consciously and on purpose. The rationalists thought that lawbreakers should be punished and that their punishment should fit the crime they committed.

The other kind of reformers were the *humanitarians*. They believed the law should be humane—in other words, that it should be caring and understanding. They believed that people often acted for reasons that they didn't understand or because of circumstances that they couldn't control. William Bradford, the grandson of the first governor of Massachusetts, wrote in the late 1700s that crime came not from evil or from bad intentions but "from ignorance, wretchedness, or corrupted manners," and that "in a country where these do not prevail, moderate punishments, strictly enforced, will be a curb as effectual as the greatest severity."

In the beginning, then, prison was itself an alternative to the colonial purpose of simple **retribution**. Rather than inflict a direct and perhaps quickly forgotten punishment, Americans would isolate their offenders from the rest of the population and give them the opportunity to better themselves while they were safely away from law-abiding citizens. They blended the desire for rational punishments with humanitarian understanding.

Over the last two hundred years, people have continued to look for even better ways to deal with crime. Some of the most common modern alternatives to prison include probation and parole.

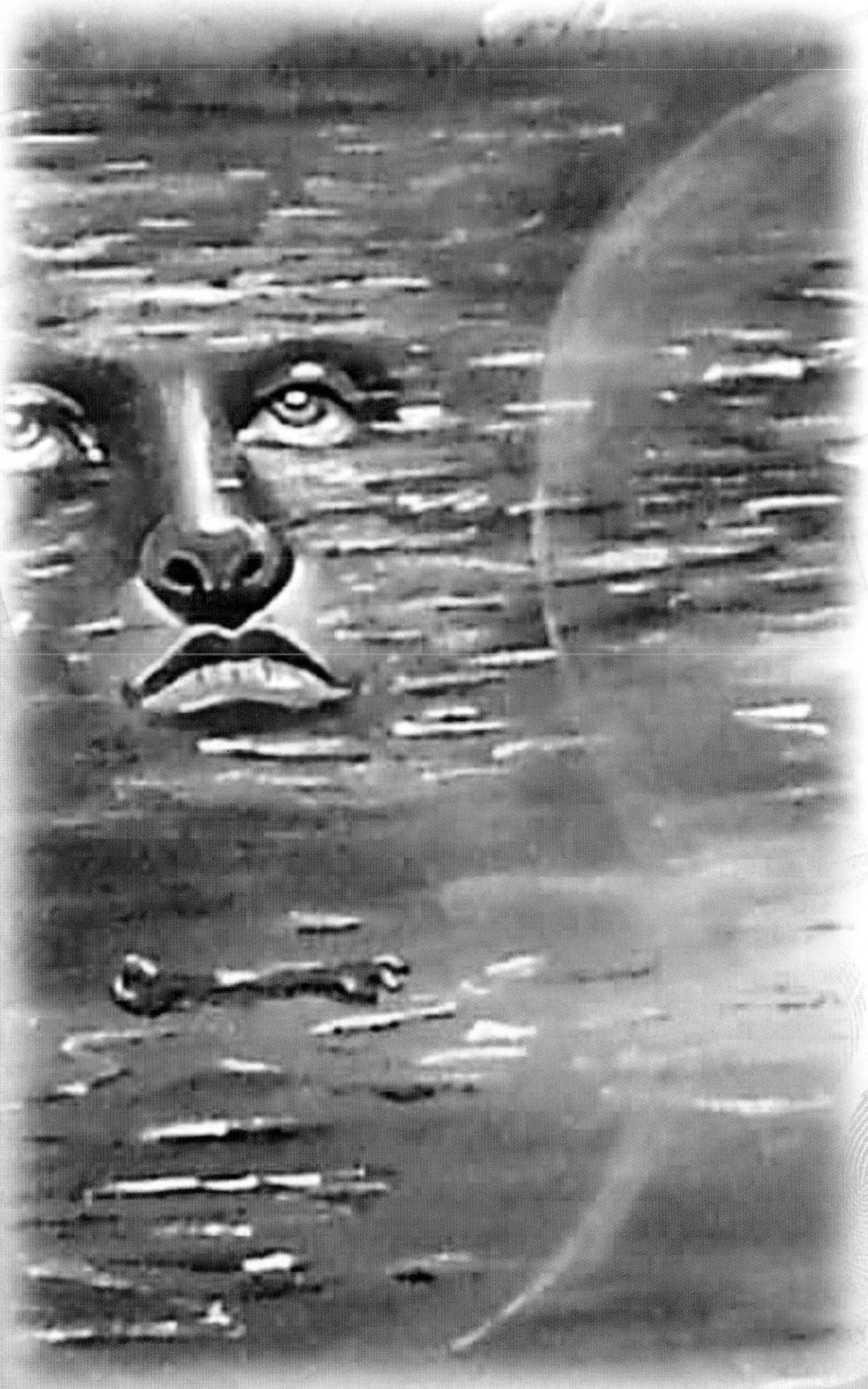

CHAPTER 2

PAROLE AND PROBATION

During the first thirty years of the United States, criminals had to serve their entire sentences in the newly established prisons, but this soon led to overcrowding. Both the rationalists and the humanitarians came up with solutions to the problem. The rationalist solution was called parole; the humanitarian solution was called probation.

Parole is a conditional early release from prison. It began informally in 1817, when prison officials, with court approval, began to let people who had shown good behavior out of jail before their sentences officially ended.

Probation also had an informal beginning. In 1841, a Boston boot maker and **philanthropist** named John Augustus asked the court to let him take charge of a drunk who had broken the law. He promised to bring the man back to court sober and employed within three weeks. When the man returned as Augustus promised he would, the judge fined him a mere penny (plus court costs, which came to less than $4) and let him go. Gratified at his success, Augustus began doing the same for others. In fact, between 1841 and his death in 1859, John Augustus saved nearly two thousand men and women from imprisonment. Soon the practice spread.

The State of Massachusetts was the first to **formalize** this sort of release in 1878, and today probation is the most widely used form of prison alternative. In 1884, Massachusetts also became the first state to formalize parole. By 1954, all fifty states had both parole and probation as part of their criminal justice systems. Almost fifty years later, the United States had a 4.5 million people on either parole or probation.

PROBATION

Today, when people are sentenced to probation, they are released into the community with a suspended sentence under the supervision of a probation officer. The word "probation" comes from a Latin word meaning "to test"—and people who pass this test by complying with the court's wishes are released from further participation in the criminal justice system. Those who violate the terms of their probation do not pass the test, and as a result, they have to serve the rest of their sentence in prison or jail. People who receive parole, on the other hand, start off in prison and serve a certain amount of time before becoming eligible for release.

The judge in each person's case decides whether she goes to prison or receives probation. These decisions depend partly on the state where she lives, partly on the kind of crime she committed, and partly on the kind of person she is.

For example, some states, like California and Texas, have serious problems with prison overcrowding. Judges in these states are more

THE TEMPERANCE MOVEMENT AND PROBATION

John Augustus, whom many consider the "father of probation," was very much influenced by the Temperance Movement. One of his intentions was to keep people from drinking. ("Temperance" means "restraint in the use of or abstinence from alcoholic liquors.") In the early 1800s, Americans drank quite heavily. Many workers spent much of their money on alcohol. Some blamed many of the country's problems, such as joblessness and domestic violence, on drinking. Speakers began traveling all over the United States talking about the dangers of alcohol and encouraging people to sign pledges not to drink. By 1838, a million people had signed.

likely to consider probation in order to keep the prison population down. Judges in states without these problems, however, are more likely to incarcerate people, especially those convicted of more serious crimes.

Judges also consider the type of crime a person has committed. Generally speaking, those who commit crimes against property, like robbery or burglary, are more likely to receive probation than those who commit crimes against people, such as assault or murder. People considered nonviolent or at low risk of either fleeing or repeating their crime also have a greater chance of receiving probation.

Finally, judges think about the kind of person they're sentencing and whether or not he has been in trouble with the law before. John Augustus, for example, was very particular about the people he offered to help. He would ask them questions and look into their backgrounds, checking on their habits and the kinds of friends they had. Also, he only dealt with people who were in trouble with the law for the first time. Because of the

A person on probation may need permission to get married.

care he took, only ten of the two thousand people he helped ever violated his trust.

Today, the courts don't have the money, the time, or the personnel to check on everyone as closely as Augustus did, but first offenders are still prime candidates for probation, just as they were when Augustus was alive.

Besides meeting regularly with their probation officers, people on probation have to meet certain conditions in order to remain out of prison. These conditions differ somewhat from state to state, but generally they encourage probationers to obey the law, stay away from other people who have had trouble with the law, and support any dependents they may have. The conditions often include the requirement that probationers tell their probation officers where they live and let the officer know if they move. Often, probationers must get permission before leaving the court's *jurisdiction*. A probationer may have to agree to submit to a search of her car, her home, or herself at any time. Some may need permission to get married, apply for a driver's license, or take out a bank

Today's courts don't have the time to give offenders individualized attention.

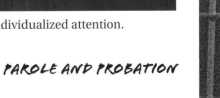

Women in prison may have very different needs and experiences than male prisoners.

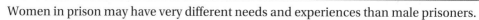

WOMEN IN PRISON: SYSTEMS OF INEQUALITY?

Although women in American prisons have very different needs and experiences than men, they face the same practices, receive the same services, and live in the same kind of facilities that were designed for men. Few prisons, for example, provide child-care services or even have facilities for visits with children. Also, the vocational training offered in prison tends to emphasize traditional, low-paying jobs for women. Canadian prisons, on the other hand, have nontraditional job training as well as a certified trade school. Women in Canadian prisons receive education, addiction and medical treatment, parenting classes, and three months of training in nontraditional jobs. In 2003, however, Canada, with a population of 32 million, had only 309 female inmates, while the United States, with almost ten times as many people, had 100,000.

loan. In addition, many also have to pay a supervision fee. Pennsylvania, for example, charges each probationer $25 a month.

The length of probation also varies, depending on the state where the probationer lives and the crime he committed. In Illinois, people receive one year of probation if they commit a misdemeanor and thirty months if they commit a felony, while Texas law says only that probation must be less than ten years.

Some people think that probation is the best of punishment for most people who have been convicted of nonviolent crimes. Nancy Martin, the former chief probation officer of Cook County, Illinois, said, "When you or I talk about jail, it's the most horrifying thing in the world because we're employed, because we have families, because our reputations

For some people, the responsibilities of a nine-to-five job may seem more horrifying than imprisonment.

mean something to us. Unfortunately for a lot of the people we deal with, those aren't really considerations, and jail really isn't the most horrifying thing. The most horrifying thing for a lot of our clients is that they would have to live my life: Get up at 5:30 in the morning, go to work, be responsible for their own upkeep and their own welfare, have to provide some type of monetary relief to their families and be held accountable." Probation forces offenders to take this kind of responsibility. It forces them to be accountable. After all, in prison, people don't have to work for their food or a place to sleep. These are given to them. Being in prison doesn't help teach people about personal responsibility. Being out on probation does.

Probation serves several other important purposes. First, it keeps people convicted of *petty* crimes out of prison and away from more

If nothing else, people in prison have a free place to sleep.

Probation offers an alternative to the shame of imprisonment.

dangerous criminals. Second, it helps people avoid being **stigmatized** as criminals. For example, people on probation can often remain in their current jobs and lead what appear to most people to be average, normal lives. Third, since they're working and providing for themselves and their families, they have a more positive self-image. Finally, because probationers do not go to prison, probation is a very practical way to ease prison overcrowding. To many people, probation is "the one correctional treatment program that seems to work."

Probation also helps society as a whole because it reduces the ever-growing cost of prison. Although it's certainly imperfect, probation provides a way to keep track of people who have committed a crime but who don't necessarily need to be incarcerated.

PAROLE

People who receive parole are already in prison. In general, people who don't receive probation from the judge have committed more serious crimes than those who do. Whether they receive parole, however, will depend on a number of factors. Sometimes people are paroled because of good behavior. Many states, for example, allow prisoners the opportunity to leave fifteen days early for every month they serve without causing trouble. This knowledge often encourages prisoners to behave well in the hope of getting out more quickly.

Often, though, the decision to grant parole must come from a parole board. Each state in the United States has its own parole board. The board in Ohio, for example, has nine members appointed by the state's governor. In Quebec, a province of Canada, the parole board has eleven permanent members and sixty-seven part-time members, all of whom are appointed by Canada's solicitor general, who is the nation's chief law officer.

When a board has a parole hearing, the members of the board interview the inmates and read their files to determine whether to release them. More than thirty states also allow the victims or their relatives to appear before the board, and twelve others allow them to submit written

statements. In addition, the boards take into consideration the crime an inmate committed, the length of time she has already served, her age, her previous criminal history, her use of drugs (including alcohol), and her record in prison. Finally, American parole boards use guidelines developed by the U.S. Board of Parole to help them make their final decisions. The guidelines not only help boards make more **objective** decisions, they also help them defend their decisions to the public. The parole then has to be approved by the governor before it becomes official and the inmate is released.

Sometimes even murderers are set free after a parole hearing. This is often because many murders are "crimes of passion." In other words, they are committed in a jealous rage against someone the murderer loved or used to love. Many believe that such a murderer is unlikely to murder again and is therefore not dangerous. In 1993, for instance, Jean Harris was paroled after serving twelve years of a fifteen-year-to-life sentence for killing her lover. In 2004, the first year that Arnold Schwarzenegger was governor of California, he approved the parole of forty-eight convicted murderers. The previous governor had promised to keep all convicted murderers in prison for life and had pardoned only eight murderers in five years. But Schwarzenegger's legal secretary says that, unlike the previous governor, Schwarzenegger "is a governor who believes people can reform and be reformed."

People released on parole are not free, however. Just as people on probation have certain rules they must follow, so must people on parole. To be released, they must sign an agreement to follow these rules of behavior. If parolees violate these rules, they are sent back to prison. In South Carolina, for instance, a parolee must agree to these standard conditions:

1. To see his parole officer no later than 8:30 A.M. on the day following his release.
2. Not to change his residence without notifying his parole officer.
3. To allow his parole officer to visit him at home or at work at any time.
4. Not to use alcohol or even to enter a bar.
5. To submit to drug testing.

Parole boards evaluate the details of a crime to make their decisions.

6. Not to possess or purchase firearms or knives.
7. Not to associate with anyone with a criminal record or with anyone his parole officer tells him to avoid.
8. To work diligently at a lawful profession.
9. Not to violate any laws and to contact his parole officer if he's arrested or even questioned by a police officer.
10. Not to leave the state without permission from his parole officer.
11. To pay a supervision fee.

Depending on his crime, he may also face additional, special conditions. Sex offenders, for instance, may be required to stay away from schoolyards or playgrounds.

The amount of time someone must *abide* by these conditions varies from state to state. Indiana has a maximum of one year. In neighboring Illinois, a parolee must remain under supervision for one to three years, depending on the crime she committed. Parolees in California who had received a life sentence might have to remain under supervision for up to seven years.

Often, the state will do what it can to help people released on parole succeed. Sometimes all it takes is something very simple and basic. Take Charles Balkcom, for instance. After he was paroled from prison in Georgia, he landed a job as a cook at a local Wendy's. Full-time work is a vital factor that helps people succeed on parole. Unfortunately, Charles lived five miles away from his new job, and he had to walk back and forth every day. Naturally, this lessened the chance that he could keep the job.

But James Williams, the chief of the Milledgeville Parole Office, had an idea. Williams had previously worked for the county sheriff's office, and he knew that the county collected unclaimed bicycles. He arranged for some of them to be fixed up and given to parolees like Charles, who was then able to ride those five miles rather than walk. Not only does this program help people like Charles stay out of prison, it also saves the state money. After all, parolees who reenter prison cost Georgia $18,000 a year.

PROBATION AND PAROLE'S RISKS

Of course, giving a convicted criminal probation or granting a prison inmate parole is always risky. Neither the judge nor the parole board has any guarantee that the person will never commit another crime. In 1981, for instance, the famous American author Norman Mailer championed the release on parole of a criminal named Jack Henry Abbott—but Abbott's parole proved to be far from successful.

Abbott had spent most of his life in jail and at the time was serving a nineteen-year sentence for murdering another inmate. In the late 1970s, he had begun sending letters to Mailer, who found Abbott to be an excellent writer. Those letters became a bestselling book called In the Belly of the Beast. In the introduction to that book, Mailer wrote, "not only the worst of the young are sent to prison, but the best—that is, the proudest, the bravest, the most daring, the most enterprising and the most undefeated of the poor." To him, Abbott was "a potential leader, a man obsessed with a vision of more elevated human relations." Mailer even went to Utah and testified on Abbott's behalf at his parole hearing. Six weeks after he was released, however, Abbott committed another murder, stabbing a young actor in the heart and leaving him to die on a New York City sidewalk. He was returned to prison, where he was never granted parole again. He was found hanged in his cell in February 2002.

PROBATION AND PAROLE'S REWARDS

On the other hand, not every parolee ends up like Jack Abbott. For Mike Noland, the prison alternatives of probation and parole changed his life completely around and helped him become a better person.

In 1992, Mike punched a man so hard he almost killed him. As a result, he was convicted of second-degree assault. The judge gave him

Community service may be a part of both parole and prison sentences.

probation, but Mike soon violated it, and in 1999, he was sentenced to five years in prison. After serving two years of his sentence, he received parole. One of the conditions of his parole was that he work at the Honolulu Salvation Army's Adult Rehabilitation Center. There he met a woman named Tracy, who told him of her plan to go to Kenya where many of the children and young people had lost one or even both parents to AIDS. He and Tracy fell in love, and they got married in April of 2003.

Even though he was still on parole, Mike was able to join Tracy for three months on her trip to Kenya in August of that year. Tracy said, "We feel so honored for this opportunity. . . . It's really hard to leave the island if you're on parole."

Mike also felt very lucky. "Every day I'm showered with miracles," he said. "I have incredible peace and joy helping others."

Tommy Johnson, the administrator of the Hawaii Paroling Authority, admitted that it was "really unusual" to allow a parolee to leave the country, but he added that "the only reason we considered it is because he's *vouched* for by the church and some community members. This is his chance to give back." He said that Mike's history of parole had been good and that he had abided by the terms of his parole. While in Kenya Mike had to phone his parole officer in Honolulu every two weeks, and he had to return to Hawaii after ninety days. "We have some success stories," said Johnson, "but you don't often hear about them."

For some people, just staying out of prison or getting out of prison is enough to keep them from committing more crimes. Other times, however, offenders need more to help them succeed.

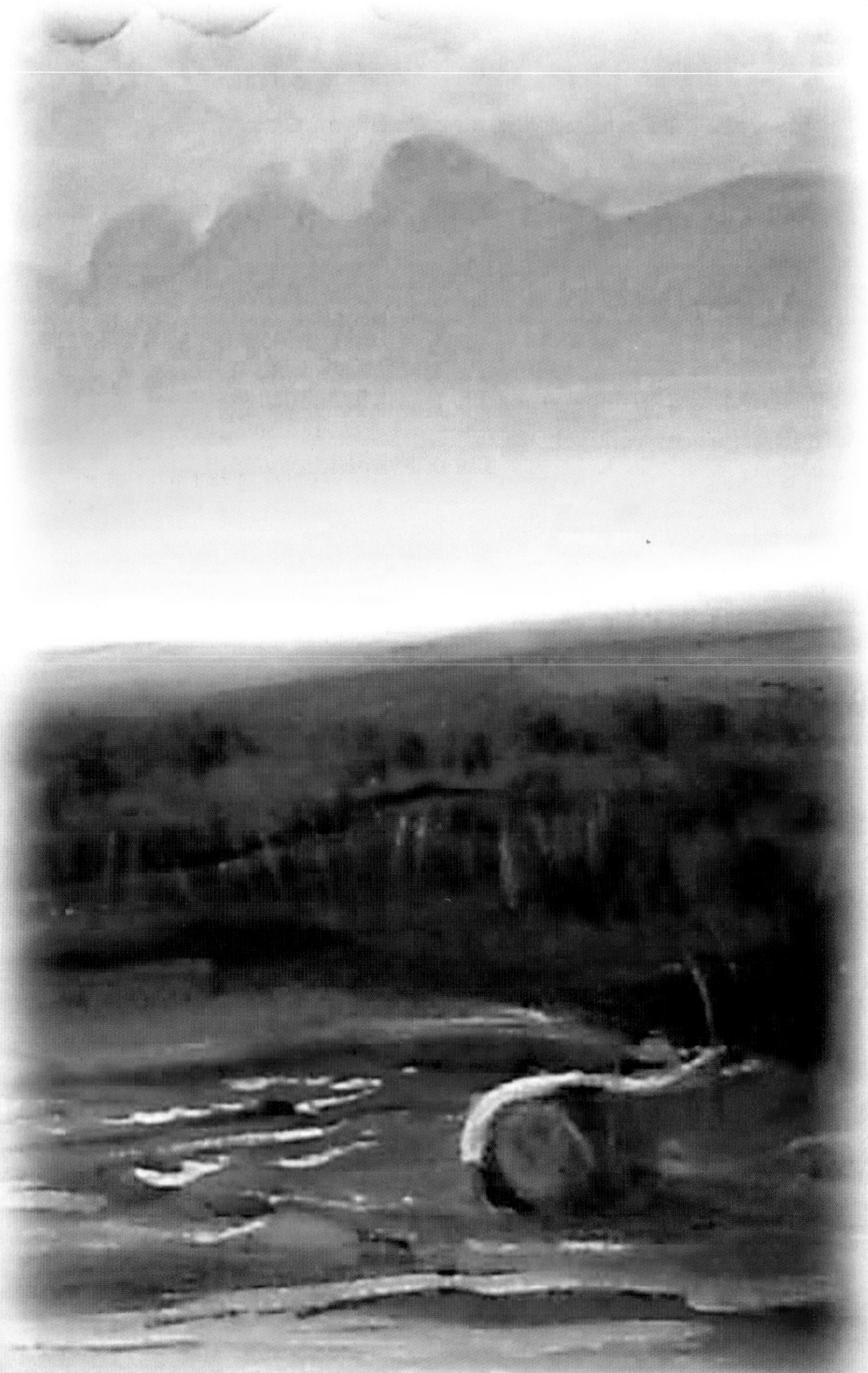

CHAPTER 3

REHABILITATION

Back in 1841, when James Augustus asked the court to let him take charge of a drunken prisoner, he didn't intend to let the man just go free and do whatever he wanted. Augustus wanted him to change his life so that he wouldn't end up in court again. Today we call this sort of change rehabilitation.

Rehabilitation helped change Antonio, a former drug dealer from New York City. When he was a teenager, he sold cocaine and heroin to support his own habit. "I had the drugs," he says. "I had the money. I got what I wanted when I wanted it."

But then he started getting arrested. He'd serve his time, but every time he got out, he just went back to selling drugs. Finally, after he was arrested for the sixth time, he met Gilbert Acevado. Like Antonio, Gilbert was Hispanic. Their similarity helped Antonio to relate to him. Gilbert had been a police officer who had also been addicted to cocaine. After he got kicked off the force, he went through treatment and became a counselor for young men like Antonio. Antonio said, "He told me that I really do need help because I'd been in jail so many times."

Instead of going to prison, Antonio entered the Drug Treatment Alternative to Prison program. As a result, Antonio is drug-free and finishing school.

Rehabilitation often goes hand-in-hand with parole and probation. It may take place in prison before release, or it may take place outside prison after release. It may also come as a combination of these. Many parole and probation agencies have special units or officers trained to help restore specific kinds of offenders to a useful life outside prison walls.

ILLEGAL SUBSTANCE-ABUSE TREATMENT

Because drug abuse is the single biggest problem among those on parole or probation, many offenders are sent to substance-abuse treatment programs. More than half of the people arrested in the United States test positive for drugs. In some cities, that number is closer to 80 percent. More than three-quarters of people arrested say they've used drugs at some point in their lives, and more than one-quarter say they were on drugs at the time they committed their crimes.

Drug treatment usually begins by getting the offender off the drug (or drugs) he is using. Often people are treated with other weaker and less addictive drugs. One such drug is called **methadone**, which is often used to help heroin users. Another is Clonidine, usually used to treat **hyper-**

ALCOHOLICS ANONYMOUS

Alcoholics Anonymous (AA) began in the 1930s. Its founder, William Wilson, found it was easier for people to stop drinking if they became part of a community in which each person could relate his own story of drunkenness and how he turned away from it. Wilson developed a twelve-step program to stop people's addiction to alcohol. It begins with people admitting in public—to themselves as well as to others—that they are alcoholics. AA provides "an important social network through which members learn appropriate behavior . . . and become involved in various (nondrinking) leisure activities with other alcoholics."

tension, but that can also relieve many of the symptoms of heroin withdrawal.

Many states place inmates in a ***therapeutic*** community (TC), which provides a highly structured environment to help people stop their desire for drugs. People there learn to work together for a common goal and provide support for one another.

Many TCs are based on the principles of Alcoholics Anonymous where they rehabilitate on two levels. The first level is social. When an abuser first joins the group, she has no responsibilities, and the others assume they can't trust her. In a TC, people have to earn both trust and responsibility. The second level of rehabilitation is mental. Abusers have to change the way they think, act, and feel about drugs.

Some inmates agree to enter a TC because it seems easier than spending time in prison. They soon learn, however, that living in a TC is sometimes much harder because they have to face up to themselves. Henry,

 Percentage of former prisoners who complete rehabilitation who return to prison.

 Percentage of rehabilitation drop-outs who return to prison.

THE ORIGIN OF THERAPEUTIC COMMUNITIES

The first TCs were in England. They started in 1946 to treat soldiers returning from World War II. It wasn't until 1969 that the first TC for prisoners opened in the United States. While the English TC relies more on psychiatrists and corrections officers, the American version relies on the peer group and role models. American TCs also focus more on lifestyle changes and on self-image, self-reliance, and work habits than English ones.

who started taking drugs when he served in Vietnam during the 1960s, says, "I came to the program to get out faster. But I've learned to deal with myself."

Chris, another member of a TC, admits that he didn't know what he was getting into when he agreed to accept this alternative to prison. He learned that treatment "is harder than jail, but it's worth it. The longer you're here, the better it is."

Prisoners who receive drug rehabilitation in Texas, which has the largest prison population in the United States, generally start out in an in-prison therapeutic community, or IPTC. On average, prisoners stay there for nine months while they receive treatment for chemical dependencies and work together toward their common goal of becoming drug-free. If successful, they receive parole but must spend an additional year in community-based treatment. A study done by Texas Christian University in 1999 showed that only 25 percent of those prisoners who completed their rehabilitation in both the in-prison and the community therapeutic communities returned to prison, compared to almost two-thirds of those who dropped out of the program once they left prison.

Rehabilitation can save Americans millions of dollars.

Officials in New York's Dutchess County make special efforts to use rehabilitation and other alternatives to prison. According to the county's district attorney, "Not many counties in this state have the program to the extent that we do. The alternative is state prison."

One reason for these special efforts is cost. About 22,000 people, one-third of New York's prisoners, are incarcerated because of drugs, and it costs the state $650 million a year to keep them confined. That's $80 a day for each prisoner. It costs only $65 a day, however, to keep them in Dutchess County's Intensive Treatment Alternative Program. Overall, New York's drug treatment plan saves the state $32,000 a year for each prisoner.

The savings to society become even greater when someone is rehabilitated and stops using drugs and committing crimes. The Dutchess County Commissioner of Mental Hygiene says, "Breaking the cycle of addiction and despair—those are the savings you don't see."

Darlene Bought, for example, says, "Rehab was the best experience of my life." She was placed there after she violated her probation for a previous drug conviction. But because of her rehabilitation, she said, she hasn't used drugs since 1999.

Unfortunately, this kind of success doesn't happen every time. However, according to Robert Gangi of the Correctional Association of New York, substance abuse treatment is "more humane, less expensive and . . . more likely to reduce crime than imprisonment." In the Treatment Alternative Program, inmates can learn how to deal with their anger. They can also take classes toward their high school equivalency diploma and develop plans for college or a career.

TREATMENT FOR ALCOHOL ABUSE

Of course, illegal drugs are not the only ones that people abuse. Perhaps the most abused drug of all in the United States is alcohol. While alcohol itself is not illegal for adults, drinking sometimes leads to trouble with the

law. Basketball player Juwan Howard, for example, was arrested in November of 1996 for driving while *intoxicated*. His blood alcohol level was .11. Like all first-time offenders in the District of Columbia, he was ordered to enter an alcohol rehabilitation and education program. Once he completed the course, the charge was dropped.

In 2001, alcohol abuse put comedian Paula Poundstone into rehabilitation as well. Like Howard, she was driving while intoxicated. Unlike him, however, she was an alcoholic, and she had her children in the car at the time. As a result, she was arrested for child endangerment. Her children were taken from her, and she was sentenced to five years probation and six months at an alcohol rehabilitation center. Once she completed her rehabilitation, she regained her children and returned to performing.

Drunk driving is just one of the dangers of alcohol abuse.

PROHIBITION

Alcohol wasn't always legal in the United States. Beginning in January of 1920, the Eighteenth Amendment to the U.S. Constitution prohibited (made illegal) "the manufacture, sale or transportation of intoxicating liquors . . . for beverage purposes." Many thought that this prohibition would make the United States a stronger nation by eliminating what they saw as the source of so much crime and poverty. Unfortunately, crime only increased. By 1933, the country had had enough. The Eighteenth Amendment was repealed, and alcohol again became legal.

Many states have programs specifically for alcohol abusers. Wisconsin began its program in 1977 when a parole and probation officer called the Department of Corrections Alcohol Education and Treatment. He had a client who, like Poundstone, was an alcoholic. The client had violated the terms of his parole and was about to have it **revoked**, but the officer didn't want to send him back to prison. "All he really needs is your six-week pre-release treatment program," he said. "Will you take him in, provide him the treatment, and return him to me for continued supervision?" The department agreed, and the client did well. He finished his probation in 1979 and never needed supervision again.

From that small beginning, the program grew. By 1984, an evaluation of their Alternative to Revocation (ATR) program showed that it had helped keep half of those who entered it out of prison. Like other TCs, this one focuses on changing the way the people involved think and on helping them learn to live more responsibly.

Rehabilitation is often more effective than imprisonment for treating DWI.

DWI

Driving while intoxicated (DWI) is a problem in both the United States and Canada. Unfortunately, simply taking away a driver's license or giving people jail time often does little to prevent them from doing it again. Some who have their licenses taken away simply drive without them. To help prevent DWI, Baltimore County in Maryland established a DWI treatment facility. The program lasts for twenty-eight days and is paid for by the offenders (unless they can't afford it). They can live outside the facility but must return every evening. After their month of individual treatment, they must continue to participate by attending support groups and AA meetings. They must also submit to random drug and alcohol tests.

REHABILITATION FOR SEX OFFENDERS

Another group that often receives rehabilitation is sex offenders, although not all experts agree that this group can be successfully rehabilitated. Sex offenders' conviction numbers have grown tremendously in the last few years. In 1979, there were just over 17,000 sex offenders in state prisons. This represented about 6 percent of the total prison population. By 1992, that number had grown to 76,000, or almost 10 percent of the total. In some states, that percentage is even higher; in the state of Washington, for instance, 25 percent of the prisoners are incarcerated for sex crimes.

Texas has a three-part program to help rehabilitate sex offenders. First, the offender goes through an educational program in which he admits his guilt and takes responsibility for what he's done. Then a psychiatrist evaluates him to determine a personalized treatment plan. This assessment takes from three to six months. The offender then remains for another nine to twelve months in the TC learning to apply the skills he's learned.

The Phoenix Program in Edmonton, Alberta, also provides rehabilitation for sex offenders. Like the Texas program, it focuses on treating the

Sexual offenders who receive rehabilitation are not as likely to become repeat offenders.

whole person. In other words, it deals with every aspect of a person's life. It includes **psychotherapy**, education, AA meetings (since alcohol often plays a role in these crimes by diminishing inhibitions), classes in anger management, and recreation. Offenders there also learn how to plan their lives better and how to set and achieve their goals. They have to stay at least six months, though most stay for ten.

Inmates have a very strict schedule at the Phoenix Program. It includes, for example, more than thirty hours of therapy every week. For

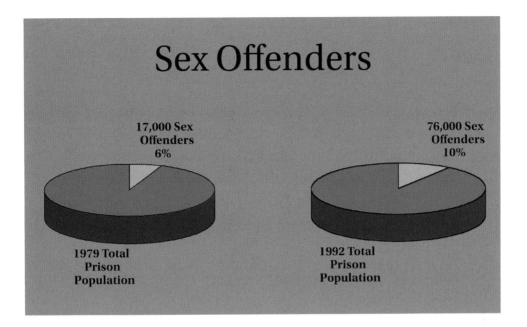

Sex Offenders

17,000 Sex Offenders 6%

1979 Total Prison Population

76,000 Sex Offenders 10%

1992 Total Prison Population

the first six to twelve months, the inmate receives this therapy while still in prison. Then, for several months after his release into the community, he comes in for four hours of therapy a night. Finally, when his therapists think he's ready, he comes in just once a week for a group session.

The Phoenix Program is considered one of the most effective in the world. Fewer than 5 percent of the people who complete their program commit further crimes.

Going through rehabilitation does not guarantee that people will no longer break the law, of course. It can, however, give them a better chance than simply spending time in prison gives them. A study of prisoners in Texas found that just 7 percent of those who completed their rehabilitation returned to crime. Unfortunately, more than half of prisoners who were given rehabilitation failed to complete it, and they returned to crime at roughly the same rate as those who did not receive rehabilitation.

Clearly, for some people, simple rehabilitation isn't enough. They need more to help them change their lives. They need something to shock them into a new way of looking at things.

Some people need boot camp.

CHAPTER 4

Boot Camp

A van full of teenage offenders comes slowly up the drive and comes to a halt. Everything is quiet.

Then, suddenly, the young men inside hear a loud whistle. A group of sheriff's deputies wearing sunglasses and drill sergeant hats begin pounding on the walls of the van, screaming orders. The men inside are dragged out and searched before they're taken away to have their heads shaved.

Welcome to shock incarceration, or as it's better known, boot camp.

According to Jennifer O'Connor in the *American Criminal Law Review*, boot camp programs "mirror the structure and discipline of military training." The first correctional boot camps opened in Georgia and Oklahoma in 1983. The mid- to late 1990s saw a steady decline in the number of boot camps. By 2000, for example, only fifty-one state-operated camps remained open.

The idea behind boot camps is that many offenders lack self-control and live only for the moment. Many of them don't know how to read, write, or think well and are only interested in their own pleasure. In a military-style boot camp, however, offenders are forced to resist pleasures. They don't have access to chewing gum, cigarettes, television, compact discs, cell phones, or even visitors. They have to deal every day with stressful situations they can't escape. They have to learn to control their anger and keep their temper. At a boot camp, they are forced to learn discipline and self-control. In return for participating, most offenders are promised early release from confinement.

MILITARY BOOT CAMP ROUTINES

The Intensive Confinement Center in Lewisburg, Pennsylvania, is a good example of what a prisoner can expect at a boot camp.

First, all inmates have to meet certain requirements before they are even admitted:

1. They must be serving a sentence between one year and two and one half years.
2. They must be first-time offenders.
3. They must volunteer to go.
4. They must be a low security risk.
5. They must be thirty-five or younger.
6. They must have no medical problems.

Boot camps teach offenders self-discipline.

Boot camp inmates have daily military drills.

Once the inmates arrive, they receive two weeks of orientation. This allows them a chance to learn about the program and to decide whether they want to participate. Those who decide they don't like it can leave during this two-week period and return to prison. The orientation also gives the people running the program a chance to see if the newcomers can follow the many rules of the camp. If they can't, they're ordered back to prison.

When orientation ends, boot camp itself begins. **Reveille** comes at 5 A.M. Once the camp guards make sure everyone is there, the inmates have thirty minutes of physical training. Breakfast is at 6:45, followed by an inspection of the living quarters. At 8:00, the inmates begin their assignments. Some have work assignments. Others take educational classes or report for counseling. At 9:15 they break for fifteen minutes of military drill. They have lunch at noon and return to their assignments at 1:00. At 4:30, they have more military-style physical training. They also have group sessions, during which team leaders work to improve the personal habits of the inmates. Dinner comes at 5:30 and lasts for an hour. Then the inmates go back to their assignments. The working day ends at 8:40. After the guards again make sure that everyone is still there, the lights go out at 10:00 P.M.

Sunday is the only day this schedule doesn't apply. That's when the offenders have time to call home, go to church, or just have some time to themselves. But at no time during their stay at the boot camp—not even on Sunday—do they have access to radios or televisions.

In Alabama, they call their boot camp the Disciplinary Rehabilitation Unit (DRU). Located at Childersburg Prison, the DRU can handle up to 180 people at one time. Camp usually lasts about three months.

In some ways, the Alabama camp has the same focus and goals as the Pennsylvania camp. Both work to get offenders to take responsibility for their own actions and to realize that what happens to them is the result of their own choices. Also, both take a military approach. The offenders wake early and do plenty of work and lots of physical training. Every day they march and have counseling.

The Alabama DRU, however, also has a very specific, three-phase educational program. In the first phase, the offenders are encouraged to realize that committing a crime is a choice they make. During this first phase, the offenders have to write out their criminal history. They have to describe all the crimes they've committed, what they did to their

victims, and what the consequences were. Often, they deny their own responsibility at first and blame their actions on everything or everyone but themselves. Eventually, though, many of them begin to see that they freely made the choice to commit crime. They begin to see, for example, that even if they were drunk when they committed their offense, being drunk was a choice they made. They learn that being poor or drunk is no excuse for crime. As one graduate of the Alabama DRU later said, "For the first time in my life, I learned to be honest with myself. . . . I learned that I have no one to blame but me."

In phase two, the offenders begin to learn ways to solve their own problems. They learn, for example, about the twelve-step program of AA and about the importance of taking their lives one day at a time. In this phase, offenders learn how to control their anger. They also start to learn more about their own strengths and weaknesses.

For many, this combination of physical and mental effort has a positive effect. According to another graduate of the DRU, "The physical training has given me a certain confidence that I can do anything. . . . The twelve steps and the classes have helped me to think better and will help me to stay away from drugs." During this second phase, offenders begin to see that if they want to, they can have crime-free lives. Many DRU officials report that they often start seeing changes in the behavior and the attitudes of offenders during this phase.

The last phase gets offenders thinking about the future. They have to write a plan about how they hope to spend the rest of their lives once they're released. They also attend lots of lectures to help them make the change from prison to the outside world. They learn that because they have been in prison, the odds are now against them. But that only makes it more important that they take seriously what they have learned in boot camp.

After the first Alabama boot camp in 1988, its graduates were asked about their experience. More than 75 percent said they felt they had changed since they started boot camp. Half said that of everything they learned, discipline and self-control would help them the most. More than half thought the program was "hard and tough" when they started, and almost 20 percent thought it was "crazy and stupid." But in the end, 75 percent believed the program was a good thing.

Offenders learn that alcoholism is not an excuse for crime.

That group began with 153 people. Fifty failed. About 14 percent were arrested again, but that is about the same as the number of probationers (17 percent) and parolees (11 percent) who were rearrested.

Texas began its boot camp program in 1989. The program had several purposes. One purpose was punishment. Another was to cut prison costs and reduce crowding. It was also intended to provide offenders with a chance at rehabilitation.

All offenders in the Texas program receive a military uniform. The purpose of the uniform is to develop a sense of pride and of belonging to a positive group. Military drills and military ceremonies make up an important part of the Texas program. Because they require the offenders to work together and to practice, they give them a feeling of discipline, unity, and accomplishment. In addition, the military aspect of boot camp demands that the offenders learn to respect authority. This is important because many experts think that a lack of respect for authority is one reason that offenders break the law.

Physical training is another important part of the program. Offenders are required to jog and to do push-ups and sit-ups every day.

They also, of course, have plenty of work to do. Most of the work at the Texas camp is farming, but the offenders also have grounds to maintain, laundry to do, and general cleaning up to do in the barracks and other buildings.

Finally, they attend a number of classes every day. Some classes deal with the dangers of drugs. Others deal with life skills like social training, stress reduction, personal and family relationships, and basic literacy. In addition, offenders receive individual and group counseling.

Sometimes boot camp can be quite effective. Tim K. is one example. At nineteen, he thought he knew everything. "I'd heard it all before, but I didn't really listen," he said. "I was hard-headed. Sure, they brought people to tell me stuff, but I just blew them off because I thought I knew it all. It was always just another person telling me how to live my life."

Then, however, he was arrested for a felony. But instead of serving four years in prison, he was sentenced to two years in Colorado's Youth Offender System (YOS).

ALTERNATIVES TO PRISON

Physical training is an important part of boot camp rehabilitation.

During his first night there, Tim was locked in a room with paper over the windows so he couldn't see outside. At two in the morning, the door opened and everyone was ordered outside for **calisthenics**.

It was a huge shock for Tim. "I threw up," he says. "They just push you and push you, and make you do all kinds of exercises and drills. It's hard when you're not in shape."

After they finished their exercises, the offenders all had their heads shaved. That night, Tim said, as he sat in his cell, he kept asking himself, "How did I ever mess up this bad?"

BOOT CAMP

Something as ordinary as pulling weeds can be part of boot-camp rehabilitation.

He stuck it out, though. He had dropped out of school in ninth grade, but within five months at boot camp, he had earned his high school equivalency diploma. He had never liked school before, but his success in boot camp got him looking forward to going to college. He wants to get married, buy a house, and become a jeweler. He says, "My mind-set before YOS was different. I always felt bored and helpless—like there was nothing I could do to get up in the world. I think I'm much better off now. I'm independent, and I'm not as much of a follower."

NONMILITARY BOOT CAMPS

Although the military-style boot camp apparently worked well for Tim, some people don't believe that boot camps need such a military approach. According to Tom Castellano, an associate professor at the Rochester Institute of Technology, "We basically know the military component by itself doesn't do much. Without the treatment and aftercare elements, we shouldn't expect too much."

James Walker agrees. He's a program director for Washington State's Department of Corrections. "We weren't really interested in shaved heads and uniforms," he says. His department runs the McNeil Island Work Ethic Camp. He says that what people like most about McNeil Island is that "it's a nonmilitary model."

McNeil has about 125 inmates, all between the ages of eighteen and twenty-eight. They spend eight hours a day doing such things as fixing fences and pulling weeds. After their first month, they have a wider range of work to choose from. They can clean up in the meat-packing center, for example, or work in the recycling yard. Some choose to do work that the nearby town of Steilacoom wants done but can't afford. Jackie Campbell, the former superintendent of McNeil, says she believes that "the behaviors and attitudes that reflect work ethics can be learned and transferred to all areas of an offender's life."

And, of course, the inmates also have classes. They learn, among other things, how to manage their anger and how to plan for life once they get out. At many boot camps, when an inmate breaks a rule, he might have to do a certain number of push-ups. At McNeil, punishment is different. If an inmate makes a racial slur, for instance, he might have to write an essay on the cultural achievements of the group he **demeaned**.

The Leadership Development Program in Pennsylvania is another boot camp that takes a less military approach. Corby Myers, the

Classroom learning is another part of rehabilitation for many inmates.

program's former executive director, says he's more interested in positive change than he is in push-ups. "We don't hire drill sergeants," he says. "Our focus is more on education than work." Although offenders there are certainly expected to have their shoes shined and to develop the ability to run an obstacle course, they spend seven hours a day in classes.

While most boot camps are only for men, a few are for women. The state of New York runs the largest one. In many ways, the women's camps are the same as the men's. The women get plenty of exercise, discipline, and military drills. Like the men, they also receive education and counseling.

CANADIAN BOOT CAMPS

Canada's experience with boot camps has been limited. Unlike American judges, Canadian judges cannot promise a reduced sentence in return for participation. This automatically reduces the number of offenders who would be interested. Also, motivation on the part of the offender is an important aspect of a boot camp's success. People who are forced to go to boot camp are much less likely to be motivated than those who volunteer. Despite this, the province of Ontario opened a boot camp called Project Turnaround in 1997. While the politicians were divided about its usefulness and effectiveness, at least one of the offenders there approved of it. People, he said, "need to start caring more about the kids. A lot of these kids are alone. They need someone who actually cares for them."

BOOT CAMPS' SUCCESS RATES

How successful is this alternative to prison? The most common way to measure an alternative's effectiveness is to find out how many offenders who finish the program commit another crime and return to the prison system. By that standard, it appears that boot camps may not be that successful. In 1993, the federal government's General Accounting Office reported that within two years of finishing the program, graduates of boot camps for juveniles were rearrested as often as parolees were. People who studied juvenile camps in Florida, Ohio, Colorado, and Alabama found the same thing. Occasionally, they found that boot camp graduates were rearrested more often than parolees. Maryland closed its boot camp in 1996 because there was no evidence that it kept people from committing crimes again once they graduated. Colorado, North Dakota,

and Arizona have closed their programs, while Florida and California are cutting back on their programs.

But many continue to believe in the effectiveness and importance of boot camps. Terry Stewart, the former director of the Arizona Department of Corrections, argues that the camps are simply too short. "It's unreasonable to expect magic in 120 days, when every other socializing institution in an offender's life, up to age eighteen, has failed," he says.

Corby Myers, formerly of the Pennsylvania's Leadership Development Program, thinks that it's not enough to look at the number of graduates that return to crime. "I don't think that's the way to go," he says. He thinks people would be better off measuring the improvements people in boot camp have made in dealing with anger and stress. According to Myers, the more important question is, "Have we made an impact on this kid, on his ability to cope?"

In his book *Boot Camps*, James Anderson argues that these camps have several advantages for offenders. First, boot camps give participants what he calls "positive attitudinal changes." They teach offenders that they are not criminals, just people who made mistakes. It also teaches them that if they change their lifestyles, they can be crime-free. Second, Anderson says boot camp participants receive many advantages that prison doesn't give. For example, in boot camp, offenders receive both individual and group counseling. They also learn to have a greater respect for the law. Parolees, on the other hand, have spent time in prison with hardened criminals, which Anderson says has a negative effect. Time in prison, he says, "exposes offenders to behaviors and experiences that reduce their chance" of doing well in society.

Many think the key to a successful boot camp is for offenders to continue receiving care after they graduate. People who graduate from the Lakeview boot camp in New York State, for example, receive six additional months of care and support. Cheryl Clark, who heads the boot camp program for the New York Department of Correctional Services, says, "If your program doesn't include an aftercare program, you're only kidding yourself. If you don't do follow-up with them, they will continue to screw up." According to an Arizona probation officer, "Boot camp is the start. It strips down the offender, takes down their defenses, and they

FEDERAL BOOT CAMPS CLOSED

In February 2005, the U.S. government announced it would close its three boot camps in June of 2005 because it had decided the camps were no more effective than prison in keeping offenders from committing further crimes. Harley Lappin, the director of the Federal Bureau of Prisons, said the move would save the bureau more than $1 million a year. This decision did not affect state camps.

become ready for change. The [aftercare] program builds them back up . . . puts on the finishing touches. It helps give them the individual skills they need to survive."

Numbers and statistics, though, only tell part of the story. While people can certainly argue about how effective boot camps are in general, there's no denying that the experience has had a positive effect on many individual offenders. As Gail Gethman, former director of the Manatee County camp in Florida, says, "If I can get even one kid to hesitate before he does something wrong, that's a success." And Timothy Hoover, a federal public defender in Buffalo, New York, says that boot camps are "far more beneficial than having someone just sit [in prison] for twenty-four to thirty months. The impact may be slight, but it's there," he says. "I never see any of [my boot-camp clients] again."

Ronald Moscicki, the superintendent at Lakeview, tells this story about the individual success a boot camp graduate can have. He was having dinner at a New York City restaurant when one of the cooks approached him and snapped to attention.

The cook was a graduate of Lakeview.

Learning a trade offers inmates other options after their release.

"She's telling us how great she's doing, then she starts bringing all her coworkers and her boss over to meet us," Moscicki said. "It absolutely amazed me: Bringing everyone over to meet her prison guards." A year later, he said, he went back to the restaurant and learned that its manager had hired three more Lakeview graduates. "If they're all like her," the manager said, "give me all you've got."

But what about people who don't need rehabilitation? What if an offender doesn't need something as drastic as boot camp? What if, like probationers, they aren't dangerous enough to send to prison, but the judge believes their crimes were serious enough to merit some kind of punishment?

For those people, another alternative may be the best approach—community service.

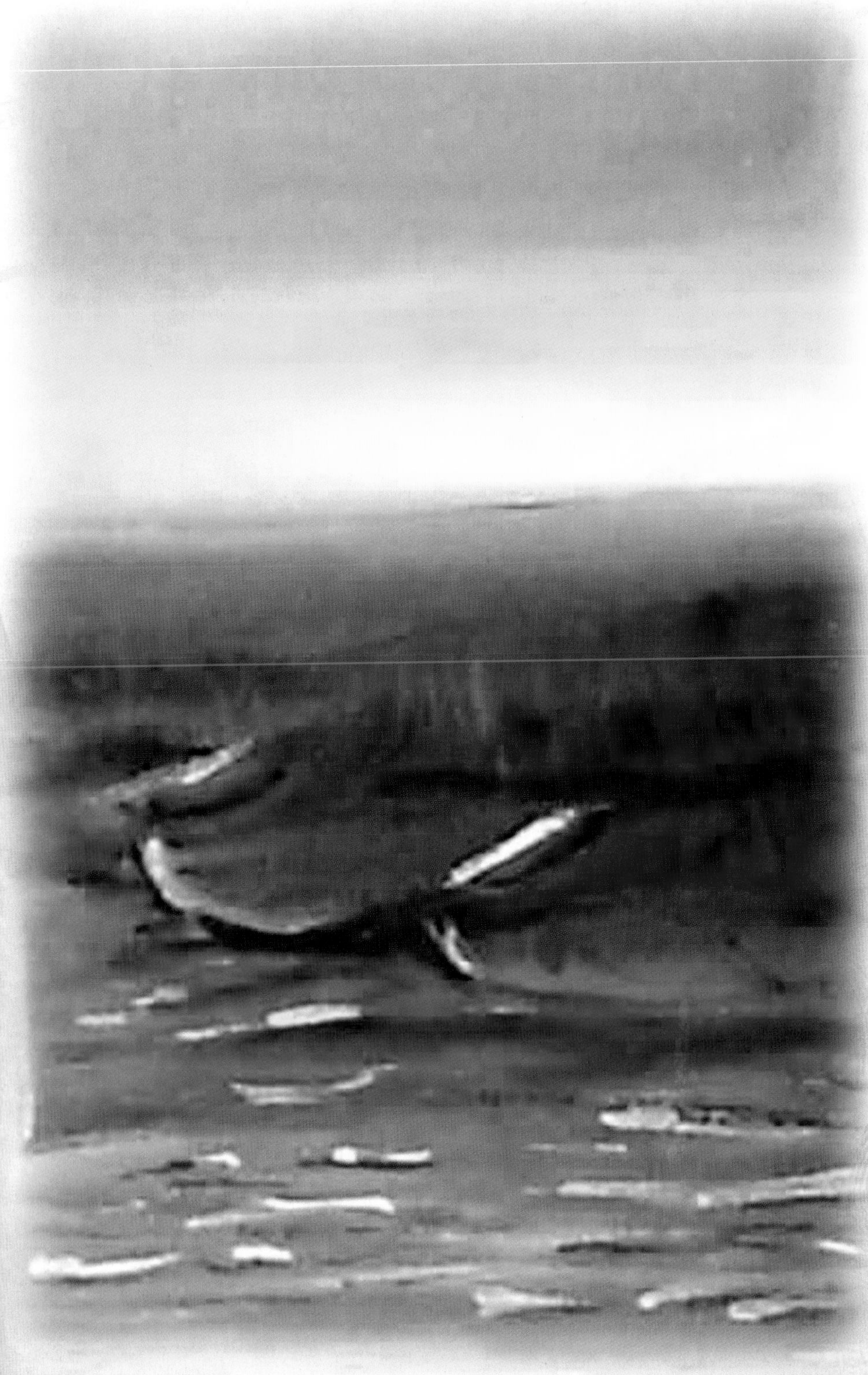

CHAPTER 5

COMMUNITY SERVICE

When a tornado hit a small town in southern Minnesota, these individuals reported to the worst areas and removed the fallen trees. They put up temporary shelters and helped the residents dig through the rubble to find their belongings.

In Quincy, Massachusetts, they listened carefully as the producer of a neighborhood theater group explained the kind of sets he wanted for a new play. Then, after a short demonstration on how to build props, they went to work. By Friday night, the props were finished, and as a reward they were given free tickets for Saturday morning's opening performance.

In Oregon, thirty of them went out in ten-degree weather to load clothing and canned goods onto a truck. Later, they helped stuff envelopes, hang banners, and hand out posters to downtown businesses, all to help raise money to build a homeless shelter.

In each of these instances, the individuals involved were offenders sentenced to community service. Rather than just sitting around in a prison cell arguing about which television show to watch or what video game to play, they're out helping people and making a positive difference in the towns and cities where they live.

THE HISTORY OF COMMUNITY SERVICE

The idea of prisoners doing work is not new; it stretches back thousands of years. The Romans, for example, often forced prisoners to build roads. In the 1600s, criminals in England were sometimes ordered to serve in the navy or were sent to America as **indentured** servants. Indeed, labor was part of prison from the very beginnings of the United States, and even into the twentieth century, many prisoners worked on "chain gangs," which were groups of men chained together and taken out of prison during the day to work on roads and in the fields.

What made community service new and different was that the work was no longer part of being in prison. It was now an alternative to prison.

Community service as we know it today began in California in 1966. When poor people there were unable to pay their traffic fines, judges started putting them to work rather than just sending them to jail. Soon judges there started giving other nonviolent offenders the same kind of sentence. From California it spread to the rest of the country. Before long, offenders were doing all sorts of work in the community. Some answered phones. Others raked leaves in city parks or picked up litter in playgrounds. Thousands of people worked at nursing homes or hospitals instead of spending time in jail. Six contractors in Nebraska who had

The Romans often used prisoners as slaves.

been convicted of rigging construction bids received community service as parts of their sentences. One was ordered to establish a program to create jobs for former prisoners. Another was ordered to plan road improvements on a nearby Native American reservation. The head of a Hollywood movie studio was convicted of possessing cocaine, and instead of being sent to prison, he was ordered to make an educational film about the dangers of drug abuse.

COMMUNITY SERVICE TODAY

In Houston, Texas, more than five thousand people do community service every month. In New Jersey, that number is about forty thousand

Community service makes people work together.

offenders every day. Offenders usually work for government or nonprofit corporations, mostly during the evenings or on the weekends. "Community service is one of the best programs we have," said Nancy Martin, the former chief probation officer of Cook County, Illinois. "We are able to take people who have committed crimes . . . and have them contribute their efforts to a variety of agencies or not-for-profit groups and have them pay back something to society." In 1991, for instance, offenders in Illinois put in 1.85 million hours of community service. If you multiply that by the minimum wage at the time, which was $4.25 an hour, nonprofit organizations received more than $8 million of free labor. According to Martin, that work not only helped the organizations; it sometimes led to employment for the workers. "Community service placements have led to employment," she says. "We have good success stories."

Offenders doing community service in Ohio have repaired computers for schools, done laundry for the homeless in shelters, helped fix

Offenders may perform community service work in parks.

Some community service programs find ways to help people who have no homes.

low-income housing, and have even trained and cared for dogs for the handicapped. They've also recorded books on tape for the blind and refurbished furniture. Between 1991 and 2001, offenders in that state alone completed more than twenty million hours of community service.

In Canada, offenders who commit a crime that would get them less than two years in prison, and who are not considered dangerous, can receive a conditional sentence that must include either rehabilitation or community service. Sometimes the offenders even have to face their victims and admit guilt for what they did. According to David Daubney, who helped revise Canada's sentencing laws in 1996, this "tries to encourage a victim-offender mediation that would provide the victim answers to questions he or she may have and provide closure."

Not all nonviolent offenders are eligible for community service, however. The Administrative Office of the Courts in New Jersey, for instance, does not recommend that people with drug or alcohol problems or those convicted of **arson** or sex crimes receive community service.

One difficulty with community service is making sure that the offenders actually show up and do the work they've been ordered to do. Sometimes a court only learns that someone has not been showing up is when she's arrested for another crime. Because community service wasn't well enforced in the beginning, people didn't take it seriously.

A COMMUNITY SERVICE SUCCESS STORY

In 1979, the Vera Institute of Justice, a private public-interest organization, decided to try to change that. One of its first efforts was called the Community Service Sentencing Project (CSSP). The first offender in CSSP was a thirty-one-year-old thief named Warren. He was arrested in late 1978 for stealing a pair of pants from a New York City department store. It was Warren's twenty-fourth arrest. Most of his arrests had been for minor crimes like shoplifting. He had seventeen convictions; of those seventeen, four were for burglary and one was for robbery and assault, for which he served five years.

Warren's lawyer thought community service was a good idea. He was afraid that, because of Warren's previous record, this conviction for stealing the pants would send him back to prison. When the court's representative interviewed him, Warren admitted he had been struggling with drug addiction for fifteen years and that he had recently been in the hospital for his alcohol addiction. His wife, who was also a drug addict, was about to go into the hospital; one of the reasons Warren wanted to stay out of jail was to take care of their child.

Because he was a heroin addict, he was going to a methadone clinic. When the court officials called to ask about him, they found that Warren came regularly. And when they looked at his criminal record, they found that he had never disappeared when he was supposed to be in court. So instead of sending him to prison, the court agreed to assign Warren seventy hours of community service.

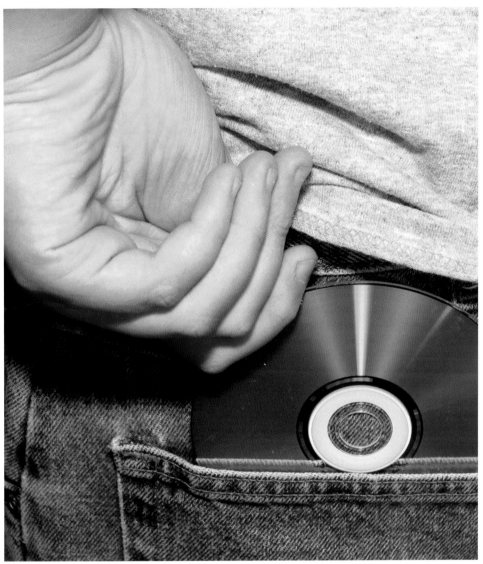

Shoplifting is a relatively minor crime that can lead to major problems.

But Friday morning, when he was supposed to start his service, he didn't show up. They looked for him all weekend long and finally found him Monday morning at his methadone clinic.

"I never thought you'd come looking for me," he said. "I just didn't think it mattered." He hadn't taken his community service sentence seriously. Afraid now that he'd be sent to jail, he agreed to start his work.

Community service work can be done almost anywhere.

Warren did complete his community service, but he needed a lot of support to do it. For one thing, he'd spent all of his public assistance money for that month. The CSSP staff loaned him some money until his next check came. They even gave him some counseling on his various family problems. In the end, Warren worked very hard on his assignment, which was to help clean up a senior citizens' center, and the judge gave him an unconditional discharge.

Because of Warren's success, the courts began giving more people community service sentences. The courts sentenced five or six people a month to service instead of prison over the next three months. Thanks to the supervision they received, these people were successful, too, and the program grew. One year after Warren was sentenced, 120 people had received community service. By the end of the next year, that number had risen to 331. This success also helped the program grow throughout New York City. It had begun in the Bronx, but at the end of 1980, it expanded into Brooklyn, and then a year later, it started in Manhattan.

Supervision from the Vera Institute was what helped Warren and the CSSP succeed. It organized the offenders into small work crews closely supervised by a foreman who was employed by the institute. The foreman checked everyone's attendance, directed their work, and drove his crew from site to site. Those who refused to work or who left early were sent back to court and usually ended up in jail. With this stricter enforcement, seven out of ten finished their community service. In addition, the project staff often found them full-time work to help stabilize their lives.

By the end of 1983, about 2,400 people were involved in the program. Most of them would have been in jail without it. Each offender had to perform seventy hours of service. Some of them cleaned nursing homes. Others painted buildings or cleaned vacant lots. All of them were under constant supervision. The program not only got needed work done, it cost much less than prison. In the early 1980s, it cost about $40,000 a year to keep one person in Rikers Island in New York City. The cost of the CSSP was only $920.

CSSP had such success that it was soon copied around the country. Between 1980 and 1995, every state in America started an intensive

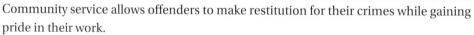

Community service allows offenders to make restitution for their crimes while gaining pride in their work.

supervised probation (ISP) program. People out on ISP meet weekly with a supervisor, undergo random drug testing, participate in treatment, and hold a job as well as perform their community service. And when combined with other alternatives, ISP seems to be effective at helping keep people from committing further crime. One study, for instance, found that offenders in California who received drug rehabilitation, held jobs, made **restitution** to their victims, and participated in an ISP were 10 to 20 percent less likely to be rearrested.

As we've seen, community service worked better when the offenders were watched during the hours when they were supposed to do their service. In other words, it worked better when the offenders had some kind of part-time supervision. Officials wondered if there was a way to extend this idea. Was there a middle ground between watching someone twenty-four hours a day and not watching them at all?

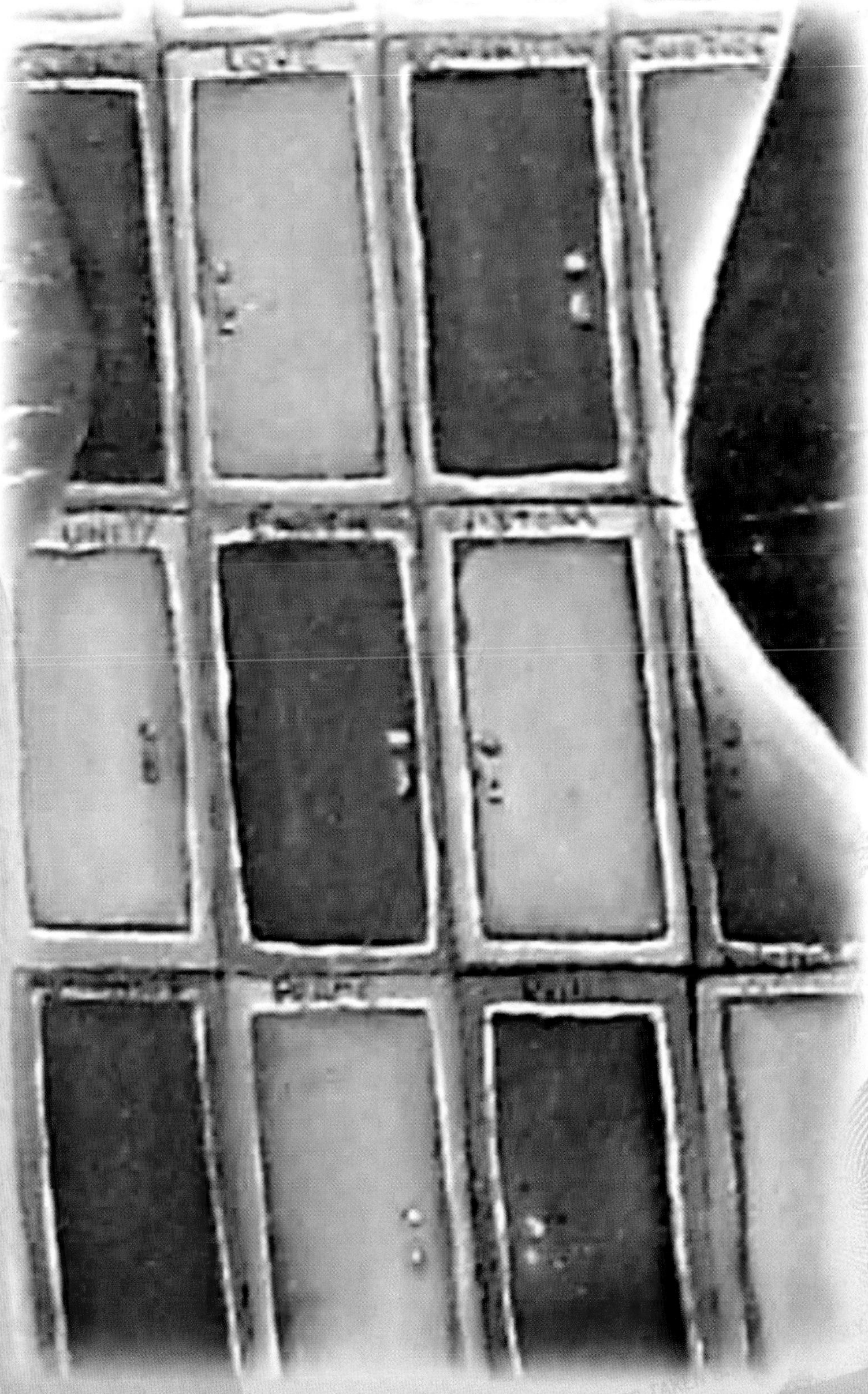

CHAPTER 6

Day Reporting and House Arrest

In 1999, Mary T. was arrested for the fourth time. But should she be sent to prison? If so, what would happen to her three children? As an alternative to prison, the judge sentenced her to the local day-reporting center. She had to go there for eight hours every day. While she was there, she took anger-management classes and received treatment for her drug addiction. She also took educational classes and got job training.

"I either had to finish this program successfully or go to prison for 24 months," she said. "At first, I thought I couldn't do it for several reasons. However . . . I'm currently taking the official GED tests and I'm hoping to receive my diploma in May. I have attended substance abuse treatment and am still going to [Alcoholics Anonymous] meetings at the day reporting center, which really have assisted in my recovery program. I truly believe my life has changed for the better. . . . I will not leave the center exactly as I came."

DAY-REPORTING CENTERS

Some people, like Mary T., don't need full-time incarceration, but they do need some kind of supervision. One solution to this problem is the day-reporting center. The first ones opened in Connecticut and Massachusetts in 1986. If placed on day reporting, parolees and probationers must report to their centers for a certain number of hours every week. The rest of the week, they live on their own.

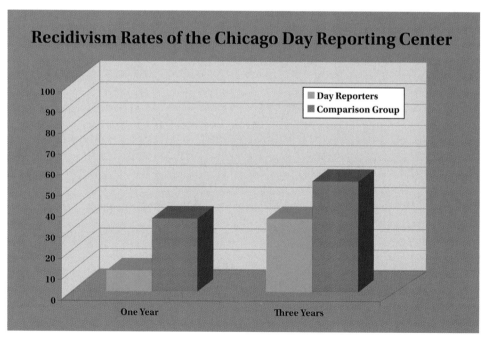

Recidivism Rates of the Chicago Day Reporting Center

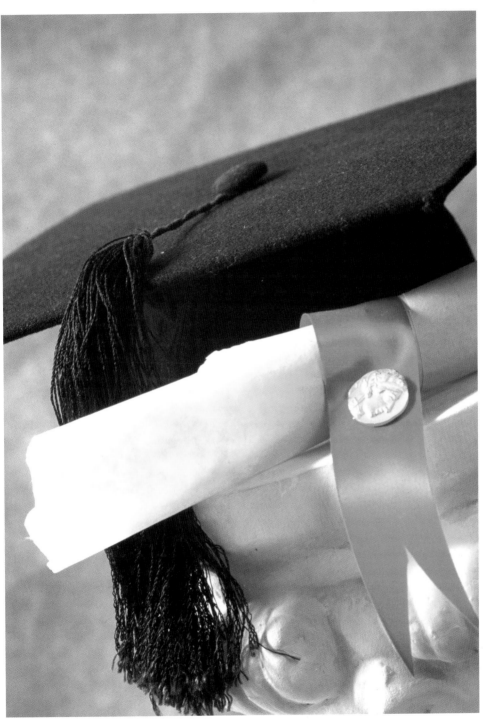

Some day programs allow offenders to earn the credits they would have received had they stayed in high school.

Day-reporting programs can offer offenders a sense of self-respect.

Day-reporting centers have several purposes. First, they give supervisors a little more control over offenders. Second, they provide access to treatment programs and other forms of rehabilitation. And finally, like all alternatives, they allow judges another option to putting someone in prison, while helping to reduce prison overcrowding and lower the state's costs.

Chicago, for example, has a day-reporting center designed for parolees who, the court believes, may be at high risk of committing another crime. This includes offenders who have been imprisoned two or more times, who have received a sentence of ten or more years, or who are under twenty-five years of age and were convicted of a violent crime. Most offenders report to the center for about six months. At first, they report every day. By the end of the six months, they might report only three or four days a week. Case managers look into their records and develop plans for supervision and treatment.

The Chicago Day Reporting Center offers many programs for rehabilitation. It has classes in anger management and provides job training and education. It also provides treatment for drug abuse. It usually has about 150 parolees at any one time. During the center's first three years, from 1998 to 2001, more than 1,500 people participated.

A study of the center done by BI Incorporated, the private corrections company that operates the Chicago center, found that graduates of the center were rearrested at a lower rate than a similar comparison group that did not have the advantages of the day-reporting center. After one year, only 10 percent of the day reporters had been rearrested, while 35 percent of the comparison group was. After three years, 35 percent of the day reporters had committed other crimes, compared to 52 percent of the other group. BI concluded that this saved the state of Illinois more than $3.5 million over three years.

Not only did this day-reporting center save the state money, it also reduced drug use and helped the participating offenders find work. Almost 85 percent of the day reporters passed their drug tests over the first two years of the program, and about half found work. Also, when the day reporters were asked to evaluate the program themselves, they said they had a "high degree of satisfaction" with its quality and services.

A painting by El Greco of the apostle Paul, who was held under house arrest two thousand years ago.

FAMOUS PEOPLE UNDER HOUSE ARREST

The idea of house arrest is not new. Two thousand years ago, the apostle Paul was held under house arrest. In the 1600s, the astronomer Galileo, who was arrested for teaching that the earth revolved around the sun, was also put under house arrest. In modern times, two winners of the Nobel Peace Prize, Kim Dae-jung of South Korea and Aung San Suu Kyi of Burma, were both put under house arrest.

A CANADIAN ALTERNATIVE

Canada has an alternative to prison that is very similar to day reporting but in one way is just its opposite. It's called day parole. While in America, people might be sentenced to spend days at a day-reporting center, in Canada they might be released during the day on day parole and be expected to return to spend the night back in prison.

HOUSE ARREST

House arrest is another option for offenders who need part-time supervision. People under house arrest are confined to their own homes. They may leave only to go to work or to see a doctor. They may also leave to perform any community service they might have been sentenced.

In 1983, Florida became the first state to use house arrest as an alternative to imprisonment. There only low-risk offenders were sentenced to stay at home. They had to pay $30 to $50 a month to help pay the costs of

A person confined to house arrest cannot leave his home, except for specific reasons.

The cost of house arrest is much less than that of prison.

operating the program and the costs of the officers who supervised them. They also had to keep a journal of their daily activities for their supervising officers to review from time to time. One of the program's main advantages was its cost. At the time it cost Florida $30 per day to keep people in prison; it cost less than $3 per day to confine them at home.

Generally, offenders on house arrest tend to be nonviolent people. They are also apt to be first-time offenders. Most have been convicted of crimes against property rather than against people. Many of them are married and have strong ties to their families. Most are employed. Also, few of them are dependent on drugs or alcohol.

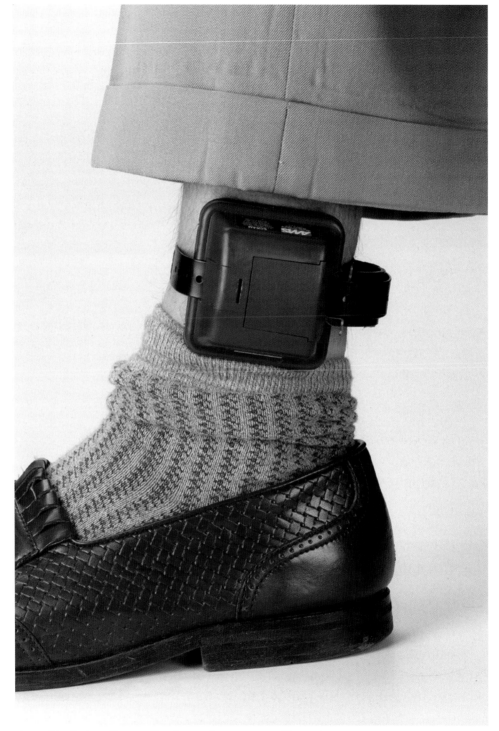

An ankle device allows offenders to be monitored long distance.

Increasingly, people put under house arrest are also electronically monitored. An electronic device attached to an offender's wrist or ankle sends a signal, usually through telephone lines, that allows officers to tell whether an offender is where he's supposed to be when he's supposed to be there. In 1987, only 826 people were electronically monitored, but by 1998, that number had grown to more than 95,000.

Sometimes celebrities are sentenced to house arrest. Martha Stewart, for instance, is a former stockbroker who used her taste in food and decorating to become a billionaire. She published her own magazine, sold her own line of houseware products at K-Mart, and even had her own television show. In the summer of 2004, she was convicted of lying about a sale of stock and sentenced to five months in prison, five months of house arrest, two years of probation, and a $30,000 fine.

Robert Conrad, best known for starring in the 1960s television series *The Wild Wild West*, was also sentenced to house arrest. When he was convicted in 2004 on drunk driving charges after he had an accident that seriously injured the other driver, he was fined $3,600 and sentenced to six months of house arrest and five years of probation.

But it isn't just celebrities who are sentenced to house arrest. It happens to average people as well. A woman in upstate New York was arrested for violating child-restraint laws in 2003 when a trucker spotted her breastfeeding her infant while she was driving her car at 65 mph down the highway. She was fined $300 and sentenced to three months of house arrest.

Criminal offenders in North America may encounter several alternatives to imprisonment. From the oldest—parole and probation—to the most recent forms of rehabilitation and house arrest, these alternatives work to find better ways to deter crime. Many people believe that punishment alone is not the most effective approach to take, both in terms of cost and success rates. As North America moves into the twenty-first century, officials and researchers continue to seek even better ways to handle the problem of crime and punishment.

ALTERNATIVES TO PRISON

CHAPTER 7

The Future of Alternatives to Prison

What does the future hold? Can improvements be made to current prison alternatives? And what new alternatives to imprisonment might exist for people in the twenty-first century?

REFORMING PROBATION

According to the Bureau of Justice Statistics, almost five million adults were on either state or federal probation or parole in 2004. In fact, 60 percent of all offenders are on probation. The Justice Department estimates that on any single day, 2 percent of the entire American population is on probation. It also tells us that the number of probationers grew 40 percent during the 1990s.

If people think they can get away with breaking a window, they may go on to commit more serious crimes.

One approach to reforming probation is called "broken windows" probation. The name comes from a theory of crime first published in 1982. According to this theory, if people think they get away with something minor, like breaking a window, they will think they can get away with other, more major things. In other words, taking care of small things will help take care of big things.

One example of what this means for probation is to have the probation officer go to the home of the probationer rather than having her come to him. In seems like a small thing, but firsthand knowledge of where and how the probationer lives is important to meaningful supervision.

Drugs like cocaine are expensive.

OTHER NEW ALTERNATIVES

Some new alternatives are interesting combinations of older alternatives. John Taylor, for instance, was convicted in 2000 of dealing cocaine. Since it was his first encounter with the law, he was tried in a special drug court.

Instead of going to prison, John went to a rehabilitation center. There he took classes in reading and math because, like many people in this program, he was unable to read or do arithmetic at even a sixth-grade level. He also received drug treatment and counseling. Then, after several months, he was allowed to go out during the day and work in the community. But he didn't work at a nonpaying community service job. Instead, he found a job at a local video store making $7 an hour. Working for money is a way of helping offenders become responsible, tax-paying citizens. At first he had to return to the center at night, but after a few more months, he was able to spend his nights at home with his mother, where his probation officer visited him once a week.

John no longer uses or even wants to use drugs. He said that things changed for him when one of his counselors told him that the women he sold drugs to were probably giving him money that should have gone to their children. "I didn't realize I was taking food out of their mouths," he said. "That sticks with me to this day." He's very glad for his experience in this program. "I knew going to prison wouldn't change me," he said, "because I'd just get out and do it all over again."

Tim Roche of the San Francisco Center on Juvenile and Criminal Justice believes that the problem with alternatives stem from how they are run. "We never addressed the fact that [a typical offender] is living in an alcoholic home," he said. "We never addressed the fact that he is nineteen years old and can't read. We never addressed the fact that he has no marketable job skills. We never addressed the mental health issues. Then we say, 'Oh, god, now you've violated your parole.' So what would have been a two-year sentence becomes a five-year sentence."

Some studies have found that a combination of alternatives like the one John received works better than just one. When offenders received

ALTERNATIVES TO PRISON

100

Prisons cost society more than just money.

rehabilitation, education, community service, and increased supervision, their chances of returning to crime dropped by 10 to 20 percent.

USING MODERN TECHNOLOGY

Modern technology may offer promising alternatives. As we have mentioned, most states already use electronic monitoring to keep track of some probationers and parolees. New technology can allow probation officers to keep constant track of their clients. For example, new electronic devices can allow offenders to be tracked by satellite twenty-four hours a day.

Another technological alternative is the automated *kiosk*. The State of Maryland started using these in 2001. Rather than report to a person, who of course must be paid for her time, offenders report to the kiosk, which records their arrival. Offenders sign in using their thumbprint and an assigned password. They then have to answer several questions presented on the screen, such as "has your address changed since you last reported?" and "do you need to see an agent (parole officer)?" Once they finish, they get a receipt with the time and date of their reporting. The kiosk is open seven days a week from 6 A.M. to 11 P.M., which makes it easy for people to report without interfering with their jobs, their schooling, or their treatment programs. If they don't report, the kiosk automatically notifies the probation or parole office.

Who knows what else the future may bring? Perhaps technology will continue to improve and bring us new and more cost-effective methods of handling criminal offenders. Research into the causes of crime may bring us new approaches to crime prevention and entirely new alternatives to prison. Society cannot afford to simply put criminals in a jail cell, lock them up, and then forget about them. We must continue to look for better ways to deal with crime, for more and better alternatives to prison.

GLOSSARY

abide: To conform to; comply with.

aneurysm: A weakened blood vessel.

aarson: The crime of knowingly setting fire to someone's property for a criminal or malicious reason.

calisthenics: Exercises.

demeaned: Reduced in worth or character.

electronic surveillance: The use of electronic equipment such as ankle bracelets to keep track of criminals.

formalize: To make official.

humanitarians: People who are committed to improving the lives of others.

hypertension: High blood pressure.

incarcerated: Imprisoned.

indentured: Bound by contract.

intoxicated: Under the influence of alcohol, drunk.

jurisdiction: Territorial range of authority or control.

kiosk: A small street booth.

methadone: A synthetic narcotic often used in the treatment of heroin abuse.

objective: Without prejudice toward one side or the other.

parole: A conditional early release of a prisoner.

petty: Small.

philanthropist: Someone who uses money to improve human welfare.

probation: A period of supervision of a criminal offender by a probation officer, in lieu of a jail or prison sentence.

psychotherapy: A treatment method for mental disorders involving talking to trained practitioners.

radiologist: Someone who takes X rays.

rationalists: People who believe in reason as the basis of action.

rehabilitation: Restoring to a useful life.

restitution: Compensation for a loss.

retribution: Punishment imposed as revenge.

reveille: The sounding of a bugle as a signal to get out of bed.

revoked: Legally withdrew something.

stigmatized: Branded as disgraceful.

therapeutic: To have healing powers.

vouched: Provided supporting evidence for something, such as a person's character.

FURTHER READING

Abadinsky, Howard. *Probation and Parole: Theory and Practice.* Upper Saddle River, N.J.: Prentice Hall, 2003.

Anderson, David C. *Sensible Justice: Alternatives to Prison.* New York: New Press, 1998.

Champion, Dean J. *Probation, Parole, and Community Corrections.* Upper Saddle River, N.J.: Prentice Hall, 1996.

Espejo, Roman, ed. *America's Prisons: Opposing Viewpoints.* San Diego, Calif.: Greenhaven, 2002.

Lin, Ann Chih. *Reform in the Making: The Implementation of Social Policy in Prison.* Princeton, N.J.: Princeton University Press, 2000.

Petersilia, Joan. *When Prisoners Come Home: Parole and Prisoner Reentry.* New York: Oxford, 2003.

Rubin, Edward L. *Minimizing Harm: A New Crime Policy for Modern America.* Boulder, Colo.: Westview, 1999.

Walker, Samuel. *Popular Justice: A History of American Criminal Justice.* New York: Oxford, 1998.

ALTERNATIVES TO PRISON

FOR MORE INFORMATION

American Correctional Association
www.aca.org

American Probation and Parole Association
www.appa-net.org

Center for the Study and Prevention of Violence
www.colorado.edu/cspv/

Correctional Services Canada
www.csc-scc.gc.ca

Federal Bureau of Prisons
www.bop.gov

John Howard Society of Canada
www.johnhoward.ca

Mother Jones Magazine: Debt to Society www.motherjones.com/news/
special_reports/prisons/alternatives.html

National Criminal Justice Reference Service
www.ncjrs.org

National Institute of Corrections
www.nicic.org

The Prison Project
boe.mars.k12.wv.us/pproject/pproject.htm

Publisher's note:
The Web sites listed on this page were active at the time of publication.
The publisher is not responsible for Web sites that have changed their
addresses or discontinued operation since the date of publication. The
publisher will review and update the Web-site list upon each reprint.

BIBLIOGRAPHY

Abadinsky, Howard. *Probation and Parole: Theory and Practice*. Upper Saddle River, N.J.: Prentice Hall, 2003.

"Actor Robert Conrad Gets House Arrest." Lancaster Online, November 26, 2004. http://www.lancasteronline.com/pages/news/ap/4/people_robert_conrad.

Anderson, David C. *Sensible Justice: Alternatives to Prison*. New York: New Press, 1998.

Anderson, James F. *Boot Camps: An Intermediate Sanction*. Lanham, Md.: University Press of America, 1999.

Bazemore, Gordon. "Community Service Helps Heal Troubled Youth." *Corrections Today* 56, no. 7 (December 1994): 74+.

Bessette, Joseph M. "Parole and Probation Have Not Succeeded as Alternatives." *In America's Prisons: Opposing Viewpoints*, edited by Roman Espejo, 145–151. San Diego, Calif.: Greenhaven, 2002.

"Breastfeeding Driver Gets House Arrest." *St. Petersburg Times*, December 5, 2003. http://www.sptimes.com/2003/12/05/Worldandnation/Breast_feeding_driver.shtml.

Browning, Frank, and John Gerassi. *The American Way of Crime*. New York: Putnam, 1980.

Bryce, Jennie. "Prohibition in the United States." *History Review*, 2000, 37.

Castellano, Thomas C. "Aftercare." *Corrections Today* 57, no. 5 (August 1995).

Champion, Dean J. *Probation, Parole, and Community Corrections*. Upper Saddle River, N.J.: Prentice Hall, 1996.

"Chronic Drunk Drivers" National Commission Against Drunk Driving, 1996. http://www.3dmonth.org/conf_12_96_exec.cfm.

Cummings, Theresa S. "Local/State Correctional Partnerships That Work." *Corrections Today* 62, no. 1 (February 2000): 22.

Cusac, Anne-Marie. "What's the Alternative?" Mother Jones, July 10, 2001. http://www.motherjones.com/news/special_reports/prisons/alternatives.html.

Dallao, Mary. "Colorado's Youth Offender System Offers Juveniles a 'Second Last Chance.'" *Corrections Today* 58, no. 5 (August 1996).

Day Parole in Canada. 2003. http://collection.nlc-bnc.ca/100/200/301/csc-scc/research_report-e/no062/html/text/rsrch/reports/r62/r62e_e.shtml.

Diiulio, John J., Jr. *No Escape: The Future of American Corrections*. New York: Basic Books, 1991.

Dodge, Calvert. *A Nation Without Prisons*. Lexington, Ky.: Lexington, 1975.

du Pont, Peter. "How the Prison System Works." *In America's Prisons: Opposing Viewpoints*, edited by Roman Espejo, 20–23. San Diego, Calif.: Greenhaven, 2002.

"Et Cetera After Life." *Time*, February 1, 1993. http://www.time.com/time/archive/preview/0,10987,1101930201-160879,00.html

Fox, Vernon Brittain. *Community-Based Corrections*. Englewood Cliffs, N.J.: Prentice Hall, 1977.

Fujimori, Leila. "Parolee's Second Chance Is a Long Shot." *Honolulu Star-Bulletin*, August 12, 2003. http://starbulletin.com/2003/08/12/news/story8.html.

Hedrick, Heather. "Bicycle Program Ensures Parolee Success." Georgia State Board of Pardons and Paroles, August 29, 2002. http://www.pap.state.ga.us/NewRelea.nsf/0/F2134417CFC5A4F085256C6700694D89?OpenDocument.

Hughes, Frank. "Howard to Take Alcohol Course, Pleads Not Guilty." *Washington Times*, December 4, 1996, p. 1.

ALTERNATIVES TO PRISON

John Howard Society. "Electronic Monitoring." 2000. http://www.johnhoward.ab.ca/PUB/A3.htm.

Klein-Saffran, Jody. "Boot Camp for Prisoners." *FBI Law Enforcement Bulletin*, October 1993. http://www.bop.gov/orepg/oreprbootcamp.pdf.

Lewis, Benjamin F., Jane McCuster, Rita Hindin, Ray Frost, and Frances Garfield. "Four Residential Drug Treatment Programs: Project IMPACT." In *Innovative Approaches in the Treatment of Drug Abuse: Program Models and Strategies*, edited by James A. Inciardi, Frank M. Tims, and Bennett W. Fletcher, 45–60. Westport, Conn.: Greenwood, 1993.

Lewis, Richard. "Boot Camp Program Promotes Discipline, Improves Self-Esteem." *Corrections Today* 56, no. 5 (August 1994): 130+.

Lewis, W. David. *From Newgate to Dannemora: The Rise of the Penitentiary in New York, 1796–1818*. Ithaca, N.Y.: Cornell, 1965.

Lin, Ann Chih. *Reform in the Making: The Implementation of Social Policy in Prison*. Princeton, N.J.: Princeton University Press, 2000.

Lipton, Douglas. "Therapeutic Communities." *Corrections Today* 60, no. 6 (October 1998): 160+.

"Lt. Governor Participates in Prisoner Community Service and Job Linkage Ceremony." Press release, March 1, 1999. http://www.drc.state.oh.us/Public/press45.htm.

Lyons, Tom. "Ontario's Boot Camp." *Eye Weekly*, March 26, 1998. http://www.eye.net/eye/issue/issue_03.26.98/news_views/coverstory.html.

Madigan, Jennifer. "Making Better Citizens, Not Better Criminals." *Capital News Online*, November 29, 2002. http://temagami.carleton.ca/jmc/cnews/29112002/n2print.shtml.

Manhattan Institute for Policy Research. "'Broken Windows' Probation: The Next Step in Fighting Crime." 1999. http://www.manhattan-institute.org/html/cr_7.htm.

McDonald, Douglas. *Punishment Without Walls: Community Service Sentences in New York City*. New Brunswick, N.J.: Rutgers University Press, 1986.

McGrew, Jane. "History of Alcohol Prohibition." National Commission on Marihuana and Drug Abuse, 2005. http://www.druglibrary.org/schaffer/LIBRARY/studies/nc/nc2a.htm.

Nicholas, Peter. "More Killers Gaining Parole." *Los Angeles Times*, September 18, 2004. http://www.latimes.com/news/local/politics/cal/la-me-parole18sep18,1,4473947.story.

Ohio Department of Rehabilitation and Correction. "Ohio Parole Board." 2004. http://www.drc.state.oh.us/web/parboard.htm.

"Parole in Texas." Texas Department of Criminal Justice. 2004. http://www.tdcj.state.tx.us/publications/parole/parole_in_tx/pit-spclzdpgms8.htm.

Petersilia, Joan. *Reforming Probation and Parole in the 21st Century*. Lanham, Md.: American Correctional, 2002.

Petersilia, Joan. *When Prisoners Come Home: Parole and Prisoner Reentry*. New York: Oxford University Press, 2003.

Posner, Richard A. "Developments in the Law: Alternatives to Incarceration." *Harvard Law Review* 111, no. 7 (1998).

Price, Joyce. "Jury Is Out" *Washington Times*, March 31, 1996, p. 3.

Prisoner Community Service. Ohio Department of Rehabilitation and Correction. 2005. http://www.drc.state.oh.us/web/commserv.htm.

Rabinowitz, Dorothy. "The Liberation of Jack Henry Abbott." Opinion Journal from the *Wall Street Journal*, February 17, 2003. http://www.opinionjournal.com/medialog/?id=100001695.

Renaissance Project Inc. http://www.renaissance-project.org.

Rubin, Edward L. *Minimizing Harm: A New Crime Policy for Modern America*. Boulder, Colo.: Westview, 1999.

Schnurer, Eric B. "Juvenile Boot Camps: Experiment in Trouble." Center for National Policy. 2000. http://www.cnponline.org/Issue%20Briefs/Statelines/statelin0200.htm.

Scobell, Beverley. "Adult Probation." Illinois Periodicals Online. Northern Illinois University, 1993. http://www.lib.niu.edu/ipo/ii930629.html.

Securite Publique Quebec. "The Commission québécoise des libérations conditionnelles." 2004. http://www.msp.gouv.qc.ca/reinsertion/reinsertion_en.asp?ndn=04&txtSection=commqueb.

Sentencing and Corrections history. Vera Institute of Justice. 2003. http://www.vera.org/section3/section3_3.asp.

Sex Offender Treatment Program. Rehabilitation and Reentry Programs Division. Texas Department of Criminal Justice. 2004. http://www.tdcj.state.tx.us/pgm&svcs/pgms&svcs-sexofftrtpgm.htm

Sex Offender Treatment Programs. John Howard Society of Alberta. 2002. http://www.johnhoward.ab.ca/PUB/respaper/treatm02.htm.

Sharp, Deborah. "Boot Camps—Punishment and Treatment." *Corrections Today* 57, no. 3 (June 1995): 81+.

Shea, William. "Successful Rehabilitation of Today's Criminal." *Freedom Magazine*. http://www.freedommag.org/english/vol29I1/page30.htm.

Stadler, Donald W. "In Wisconsin: Alternative to Revocation Program Offers Offenders a Second Chance." *Corrections Today* 56, no. 1 (February 1994): 44+.

"Status Report: Kiosk Reporting System." State of Maryland Department of Public Safety and Correctional Services. 2002. http://www.dpscs.state.md.us/dpp/kiosk_report.pdf.

Sullivan, Jacqueline. "Shattering 'Broken Windows': An Analysis of San Francisco's Alternative Crime Policies." Center on Juvenile and Criminal Justice. 2002. http://www.cjcj.org/pubs/windows/windows.html.

Tonry, Michael. "Evaluating Intermediate Sanction Programs." In *Community Corrections*, edited by Joan Petersilia, 79–96. New York: Oxford University Press, 1998.

Trapani, Carol. "Treatment Keeps Some Out of Prison." *Poughkeepsie Journal*, November 17, 2000. http://www.poughkeepsiejournal.com/projects/prison/po111700s3.shtml.

Tucker, Neely. "Parole Can Succeed as an Alternative." In *America's Prisons: Opposing Viewpoints*, edited by Roman Espejo, 139–144. San Diego, Calif.: Greenhaven, 2002.

U.S. Department of Justice. Bureau of Justice Statistics. "Correctional Populations." 2004. http://www.ojp.gov/bjs/glance/tables/corr2tab.htm.

U.S. Department of Justice. Office of Justice Programs. "State Prison Expenditures 2001." 2002. http://www.ojp.usdoj.gov/bjs/pub/pdf/spe01.pdf.

Vera Institute of Justice. http://www.vera.org/about/about_2.asp.

Willing, Richard. "US Prisons to End Boot Camp Programs." USA Today, February 3, 2005. http://www.usatoday.com/news/nation/2005-02-03-boot-camps_x.htm.

Yourk, Darren. "Cost of Prison Rising." *Toronto Globe and Mail*, October 30, 2002. http://www.theglobeandmail.com/servlet/Page/document/v4/sub/MarketingPage?user_URL=http://www.theglobeandmail.com%2Fservlet%2FArticleNews%2Ffront%2FRTGAM%2F20021030%2Fwpris1030%2FFront%2FhomeBN%2Fbreakingnews&ord=1103136748715&brand=theglobeandmail&force_login=true.

INDEX

PICTURE CREDITS

Benjamin Stewart (hardinghousegraphics.com): pp. 96, 98, 99, 100, 102
iStock: pp. 45, 89, 90
     Angie Trigg: p. 31
     Benjamin Stewart (hardinghousegraphics.com): p. 26
iStock: pp. 56, 64, 74, 88, 93
     Anita Patterson: p. 79
     Brian McLister: p. 10
     Christian K: p. 82
     Dan Lee: p. 101
     Danish Kahn: p. 50
     Dirk Diesel: p. 29
     Frances Twitty: p. 36
     Jim Jurica: p. 30
     Jonas Engstrom: p. 80
     Kevin Russ: p. 76
     Randall Schwanke: p. 99
     Rasmus Rasm: p. 59
     Roberta Osborne: p. 55
     Sean Nel: p. 33
     Steve Cook: p. 62
     Terry Healy: p. 75
Jupiter Images: pp. 11, 12, 16, 24, 25, 28, 44, 46, 48, 61, 68, 87, 92, 98

To the best knowledge of the publisher, all other images are in the public domain. If any image has been inadvertently uncredited, please notify Harding House Publishing Service, Vestal, New York 13850, so that rectification can be made for future printings.

Chapter opening art was taken from a painting titled *Choices and What Might Have Been* by Raymond Gray.

Raymond Gray has been incarcerated since 1973. Mr. Gray has learned from life, and hard times, and even from love. His artwork reflects all of these.

BIOGRAPHIES

AUTHOR

Craig Russell teaches writing at Broome Community College in Binghamton, New York.

SERIES CONSULTANT

Dr. Larry E. Sullivan is Associate Dean and Chief Librarian at the John Jay College of Criminal Justice and Professor of Criminal Justice in the doctoral program at the Graduate School and University Center of the City University of New York. He first became involved in the criminal justice system when he worked at the Maryland Penitentiary in Baltimore in the late 1970s. That experience prompted him to write the book *The Prison Reform Movement: Forlorn Hope* (1990; revised edition 2002). His most recent publication is the three-volume *Encyclopedia of Law Enforcement* (2005). He has served on a number of editorial boards, including the *Encyclopedia of Crime and Punishment* and *Handbook of Transnational Crime and Justice*. At John Jay College, in addition to directing the largest and best criminal justice library in the world, he teaches graduate and doctoral level courses in criminology and corrections. John Jay is the only liberal arts college with a criminal justice focus in the United States. Internationally recognized as a leader in criminal justice education and research, John Jay is also a major training facility for local, state, and federal law enforcement personnel.

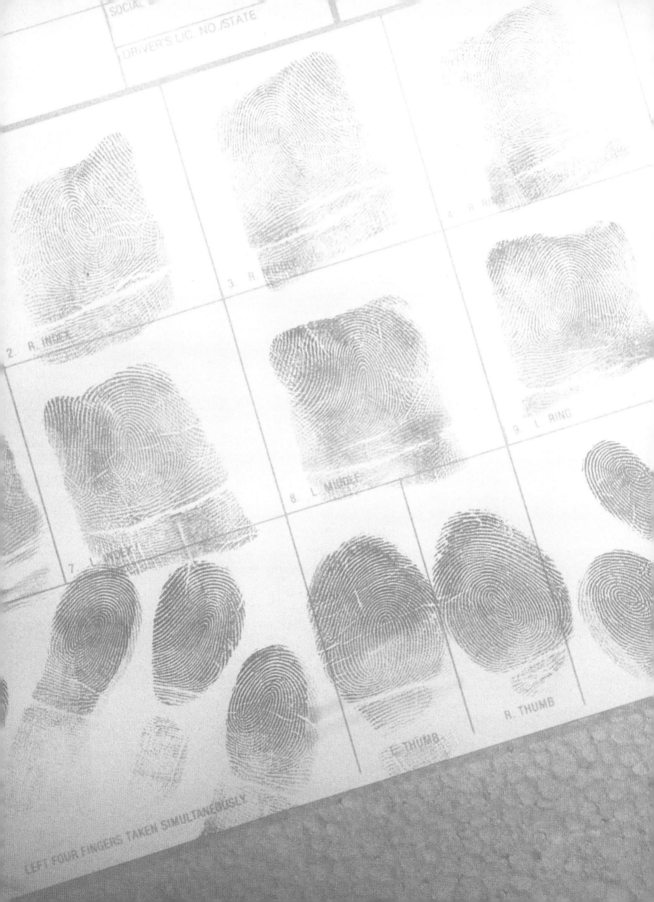